THE MOST VALUABLE BUSINESS LEGAL FORMS YOU'LL EVER NEED

—

James C. Ray
Attorney at Law

 Sphinx Publishing
A Division of Sourcebooks, Inc.
Naperville, IL • Clearwater, FL

Second Edition, 1998

Published by: **Sourcebooks, Inc.**

Naperville Office
P.O. Box 372
Naperville, Illinois 60566
(630) 961-3900
FAX: 630-961-2168

Clearwater Office
P.O. Box 25
Clearwater, Florida 33757
(813) 587-0999
FAX: 813-586-5088

Cover Design: Andrew Sardina/Dominique Raccah, Sourcebooks, Inc.
Interior Design and Production: Andrew Sardina, Sourcebooks, Inc.

This publication is designed to provide accurate and authoritative information in regard to the subject matter covered. It is sold with the understanding that the publisher is not engaged in rendering legal, accounting, or other professional service. If legal advice or other expert assistance is required, the services of a competent professional person should be sought.

From a Declaration of Principles Jointly Adopted by a Committee of the
American Bar Association and a Committee of Publishers and Associations

Library of Congress Cataloging-in-Publication Data
Ray, James C.
    The most valuable business legal forms you'll ever need / James C.
Ray.—2nd ed.
      p. cm.
Includes index.
    ISBN 1-57071-345-6 (pbk.)
    1. Contracts—United States—Forms.   I. Title.
KF801.A65R39   1998
346.7302'0269—dc21

98-3338
CIP

Printed and bound in the United States of America.

Paperback — 10 9 8 7 6 5 4 3 2 1

CONTENTS

USING SELF-HELP LAW BOOKS

Whenever you shop for a product or service, you are faced with various levels of quality and price. In deciding what product or service to buy, you make a cost/value analysis on the basis of your willingness to pay and the quality you desire.

When buying a car, you decide whether you want transportation, comfort, status, or sex appeal. Accordingly, you decide among such choices as a Neon, a Lincoln, a Rolls Royce, or a Porsche. Before making a decision, you usually weigh the merits of each option against the cost.

When you get a headache, you can take a pain reliever (such as aspirin) or visit a medical specialist for a neurological examination. Given this choice, most people, of course, take a pain reliever, since it costs only pennies, whereas a medical examination costs hundreds of dollars and takes a lot of time. This is usually a logical choice because rarely is anything more than a pain reliever needed for a headache. But in some cases, a headache may indicate a brain tumor, and failing to see a specialist right away can result in complications. Should everyone with a headache go to a specialist? Of course not, but people treating their own illnesses must realize that they are betting on the basis of their cost/value analysis of the situation, they are taking the most logical option.

The same cost/value analysis must be made in deciding to do one's own legal work. Many legal situations are very straight forward, requiring a simple form and no complicated analysis. Anyone with a little intelligence and a book of instructions can handle the matter without outside help.

But there is always the chance that complications are involved that only an attorney would notice. To simplify the law into a book like this, several legal cases often must be condensed into a single sentence or paragraph. Otherwise, the book would be several hundred pages long and too complicated for most people. However, this simplification necessarily leaves out many details and nuances that would apply to special or unusual situations. Also, there are many ways to interpret most legal questions. Your case may come before a judge who disagrees with the analysis of our authors.

Therefore, in deciding to use a self-help law book and to do your own legal work, you must realize that you are making a cost/value analysis and deciding that the chance your case will not turn out to your satisfaction is outweighed by the money you will save in doing it yourself. Most people handling their own simple legal matters never have a problem, but occasionally people find that it ended up costing them more to have an attorney straighten out the situation than it would have if they had hired an attorney in the beginning. Keep this in mind while handling your case, and be sure to consult an attorney if you feel you might need further guidance.

INTRODUCTION

THE PURPOSE OF THIS BOOK

This book is in some ways a companion to *The Most Valuable Corporate Forms You'll Ever Need*, also published by Sourcebooks, Inc. While that book concentrates on the special documents useful to corporations, this one has a broader application. It is intended to provide useful forms for all businesses, whatever their legal structure may be. Therefore, for businesses run as partnerships, sole proprietorships, corporations or other forms, this book stands alone. For that reason, it may be useful to repeat some of the cautions included in the introduction to *The Most Valuable Corporate Forms You'll Ever Need*.

It is to be hoped that this book will make fewer the occasions on which you will need a lawyer. But it may not. It will have served its purpose if it only helps you to recognize the occasions on which you do need a lawyer, and helps you to use your lawyer more efficiently.

Failing to hire a lawyer when you need one is not likely to be an economy. If, in reading this book, you discover that what you want to do is more complicated than you imagined or involves a large sum of money, then get a lawyer. If all goes well, you can complain about paying for something you didn't need after all. That's better than not hiring a lawyer and having something more serious to complain about.

Some clients believe that, having turned a matter over to the lawyers, they are released from all further responsibility. "After all," such a client thinks, "if I pay a large amount of money for my lawyer to draft a contract, why should I bore myself by reading it. It's the lawyer's job to make sure it's right."

But that makes the lawyer's job nearly impossible. You know your business and what is important for it. The best lawyer's ideas about that may be completely wrong, and he or she may attach importance to the unimportant (because it was important to the last client) and gloss over a critical factor. Use this book to know what to expect from your lawyer and why. And then read and understand the work your lawyer does for you. Make sure it works for you.

The forms in this book have been limited to those which will be usable in all states. There are other business forms books on the market which claim to be comprehensive, but include many forms (such as deeds, bad check notices, UCC-1 forms, and leases), which are unusable in many states. For example, deeds vary from state to state. Some states have very specific requirements for how the witnesses must be indicated, the form of the notary public certification, and where and how much space must be left blank for the entry of recording information. Also, each state has its own official form for filing a security interest under the Uniform Commercial Code (UCC-1 form), and some assess a penalty for failing to use the official form. Some states have specific forms for bad check notices, and have required statements and warnings in leases. It would be impossible to provide such forms for each state in a book such as this, and it would be irresponsible to include such forms knowing that they will not comply with the laws in every state.

ORGANIZATION OF THIS BOOK

The first chapter of the book deals with some general principles of contract law, and following chapters apply those principles to specific situations. Before you use any of the contract forms in this book, pay careful attention to the first chapter, especially the information about the proper execution of contracts. Depending on the form of your business—corporation, partnership, sole proprietorship, etc.—and the form of business of the entity you contract with, you will need to insert the proper signature format to make sure the proper party executes the contract and does so correctly.

Chapters 2 through 4 deal with employees and various other kinds of agents. Beginning with chapter 5, the book deals with specific business transactions—buying and selling, renting, borrowing and lending money. Chapter 9 deals with issues of liability—and how to avoid it—in connection with contract disputes and other matters. Chapter 10 contains several miscellaneous forms that may be useful in connection with all the matters covered elsewhere in the book.

The sample forms in the main part of the book are presented with information filled in for fictional businesses. The forms may be abbreviated or otherwise slightly different from the forms in the appendix in order to save space. The forms in the appendix are designed to be used *as is*, although you may need to modify them to meet your specific needs. As stated above, those included in the appendix are the forms of most general use.

APPLICABLE LAWS

This book is intended to be used throughout the United States, and the laws of no specific jurisdiction are cited or relied on in this text. While the laws of the various states vary significantly, general principles of contract and agency apply in every state. However, it may be that your specific circumstances raise a legal issue unique to your jurisdiction. For that reason and others, competent legal advice is always desirable. Especially so in the areas where the need for a lawyer is explicitly mentioned in this book, but in other circumstances as well.

How Contracts Work 1

A "Private" Kind of Law

Somewhere in the archives of Canterbury Cathedral in England is a contract, called the Accord of Winchester, that has been in force for nearly a thousand years. It's signed by King William and Queen Maude and the Archbishops of Canterbury and York. It was a bad deal for York. It put Canterbury in charge, and York didn't like it. But it's that way to this day, and nobody expects the contract to be terminated or breached. It's the law.

Even if you're not the king, when you agree to a contract, you create a law that applies to you and the other people who contract with you. It remains the law until you agree to change it, or all the obligations created by the contract are fulfilled, or it becomes impossible to enforce for one reason or another. If you "break" the law by breaching the contract, the injured party can bring in enforcement help by going to court. If the court finds that it has jurisdiction, it will interpret the contract and determine whether it has been breached. If it has, then the court will require compliance or compensation, by force if necessary.

ARE ALL AGREEMENTS LEGALLY ENFORCEABLE CONTRACTS?

Clearly, the answer to this question is "no." If you and your best friend agree to have lunch, and your friend doesn't show up, has a contract been broken? Probably not. You wouldn't expect a court to waste its time on such a trivial matter. But suppose you agreed to meet with your lawyer for lunch to discuss an important transaction, and he or she fails to make it. As a result of your misplaced reliance on the lawyer, you are seriously disadvantaged and lose piles of money on the transaction. You may think you should receive damages from the lawyer because he or she failed to keep an important promise.

How will the court know that the first lunch date agreement was trivial and the second was important enough to justify the court's intervention? It will look for the basic requirements, or *elements*, of a contract. If all the elements are there, then there is a contract, and the court will enforce it. Briefly, the court looks for the following elements (the second element, *consideration*, distinguishes the two lunch dates):

VOLUNTARY AGREEMENT

A *voluntary agreement* is created when one person makes an offer to another person who accepts it, where the parties have *capacity* (that is they are sane, sober and old enough to know what they are doing) and are not under duress or otherwise deluded.

CONSIDERATION

Consideration is something given in exchange for something else. That is, it is something "bargained for." It could be money or other property, an act (such as mowing the lawn) or even a promise to do (or not to do) something. But it must be something, however great or trivial. Courts don't like to concern themselves with the value of consideration given, reasonably thinking that "fairness" and "value" are entirely too subjective. Only you know how much you are willing to pay for your favorite rock star's used handkerchief, and if you decide to trade your house for it, as long as the other elements are present, the court won't stand in your way—or save you from yourself.

LEGALITY   As a matter of policy, the courts will not enforce contracts to do something that is illegal or, in the court's opinion, severely detrimental to the public. So if you pay someone to have your spouse eliminated, and the contracting party botches the job, don't expect the court to award damages to you. The courts even go so far as to refuse to allow professionals to collect otherwise legitimate fees for services if their professional licenses are not in order. Courts have refused to help landlords collect rent while their rental properties are in violation of building codes. This "hands off" policy is no doubt desirable, but has far reaching consequences. For example, drug dealers cannot rely on the courts to enforce contracts for the sale of illicit drugs, and so must turn to badly dressed but well armed alternative enforcement agents. This adds to the cost of drugs, and attracts undesirable people into the recreational drug business. Society must weigh the advantages against the costs of all its policy decisions.

GET IT IN WRITING

You'll notice that *writing* is not one of the elements listed above. It could have been, at least for some contracts. Every state makes some contracts unenforceable by the courts unless the contracts are written down and signed by the party trying to avoid the deal. You will hear lawyers say such contracts are "within the Statute of Frauds." They are referring to a very old English statute that has been enacted in one form or another by each of the United States, but it is misleading. The phrase has come to refer to all contracts which must be in writing to be enforceable, not just the ones you will see listed in your state's version of the Statute of Frauds.

Common examples of contracts "within the Statute" are contracts for the sale of real property, promises to pay a debt owed by another person, and contracts which will take more than one year to complete.

But most contracts are enforceable even if they are not in writing. Therefore, the usual purpose of getting something in writing is not to make it valid and legally binding, but rather to make it easier to prove that something is true. In other words, the writing is evidence, to be used in court if necessary, that something actually happened—that a promise was actually made, or an event actually occurred.

The writing doesn't have to be elaborate. It may not even have to be signed to be useful. Sometimes it is enough to have a written statement that can be proven to have been made by a particular person. If someone makes a promise to you that you intend to rely on, get the promisor to write it down. If he or she won't, then you write it down, date it and sign it. Later you can swear that you wrote it down at the time the promise was made and that your description of the promise was accurate. It's not ideal, but it may be a little better than nothing.

The two sample forms on the following pages are simple ways to get things in writing. Sample Form 1 is a simple contract form. Sample Form 2 is a contract in the form of a letter. If you write another person a letter describing a bargain the two of you have reached, and the addressee of the letter returns a copy of the letter with his or her signed consent to the terms as stated in the letter, you have a written contract. (Notice the word *bargain* which implies consideration and the other elements mentioned above.) This format is also used by people who want a written acknowledgment of some oral statement previously made by the addressee. Such an acknowledgment may not be a contract but is a signed admission that whatever was stated in the letter is true and correct.

Even if the other person doesn't sign a copy of your letter, if you send the letter by "certified mail, return receipt requested," you will at least be able to prove that you put your agreement in writing and the other party received it. If the other party can't prove he or she responded by denying the agreement, the court is likely to conclude there was an agreement as you claim.

Form 1 in the appendix is designed to allow you to insert extra pages if needed. You will note that at the bottom of the first page is the notation: "Page 1 of _____ pages." If you only need the two pages contained in the appendix, fill in the blank with the number "2," and on the second page fill in this notation to read: "Page __2__ of __2__." If you need one or more extra pages, repeat this notation on each additional page. For example, if you need one extra page, the first page would indicate: "Page 1 of __3__ pages." The second page would read: "Page __2__ of __3__ pages." The last page would read: "Page __3__ of __3__ pages."

Another way to put in additional provisions, especially after you have typed up the initial agreement, is to use an *addendum*. There is a provision on the second page of Form 1 where you can indicate that an addendum is attached. Form 2 in the appendix is an addendum form. There is a space to fill in a number for the addendum, as there may be more than one addendum attached to a contract.

In addition to a general contract form, the appendix contains two special types of contracts for specific situations. Form 48 is a contract for the sale of goods, and Form 49 is a consignment sale contract.

Sample Form 1. Simple Contract—

CONTRACT

THIS AGREEMENT is entered into by and between _____Scrupulous_____
Corporation of America _____ (hereafter referred to as
___SCA_____) and _____American Computer Consulting, Inc._
(hereafter referred to as ____ACC_____). In consideration of the mutual
promises made in this agreement and other valuable consideration, the receipt and
sufficiency of which is acknowledged, the parties agree as follows:

1.   ACC will provide SCA with ten hours of computer consulting services during the period from February 19, 1998
through February 23, 1998.

2.   ACC will provide SCA with up to five hours of follow-
up and trouble-shooting computer services for a period of one
year from the date of this agreement.

3.   SCA will pay ACC the sum of $400.00 for the services
described in paragraphs 1 and 2; to be paid $200.00 on February
19, 1998 and $200.00 upon completion of the initial ten hours
of consulting services.

4.   ACC will provide SCA with additional consulting and
trouble-shooting computer services at the rate of $32.00 per
hour for a period of one year from the date of this agreement.

Page 1 of __2__ pages

The following addenda, dated the same date as this agreement, are incorporated in, and made a part of, this agreement:

☒ None.

This agreement shall be governed by the laws of ___New York___.

If any part of this agreement is adjudged invalid, illegal, or unenforceable, the remaining parts shall not be affected and shall remain in full force and effect.

This agreement shall be binding upon the parties, and upon their heirs, executors, personal representatives, administrators, and assigns. No person shall have a right or cause of action arising out of or resulting from this agreement except those who are parties to it and their successors in interest.

This is instrument, including any attached exhibits and addenda, constitutes the entire agreement of the parties. No representations or promises have been made except those that are set out in this agreement. This agreement may not be modified except in writing signed by all the parties.

IN WITNESS WHEREOF the parties have signed this agreement under seal on ___February 12, 1998___.

Scrupulous Corporation of
    America
   Henry Hardy
_____
Henry Hardy, President

  Calvin Collier
_____
Calvin Collier, Secretary

(Corporate Seal)

American Computer Consulting,
    Inc.
   James C. Jones
_____
James C. Jones,
Vice President

  Jackson C. Jones
_____
Jackson C. Jones, Secretary

(Corporate Seal)

Page __2__ of __2__ pages.

Sample Form 2. Simple Letter Contract—

Scrupulous Corporation of America

400 West 61st Avenue, P.O. Box 19, New York, NY 10032

February 12, 1998

James C. Jones, Vice President
American Computer Consulting, Inc.
143 East 75th Street
New York, NY 10033

Re: Agreement for Computer Consulting Services

Dear Mr. Jones:

This letter will confirm the understanding reached between you and the undersigned on February 12, 1998, regarding the matter described above. We have agreed as follows:

1. ACC will provide SCA with ten hours of computer consulting services during the period from February 19, 1998 through February 23, 1998.

2. ACC will provide SCA with up to five hours of follow-up and trouble-shooting computer services for a period of one year from the date of this agreement.

3. SCA will pay ACC the sum of $400.00 for the services described in paragraphs 1 and 2; to be paid $200.00 on February 19, 1998 and $200.00 upon completion of the initial ten hours of consulting services.

4. ACC will provide SCA with additional consulting and trouble-shooting computer services at the rate of $32.00 per hour for a period of one year from the date of this agreement.

Enclosed is a copy of this letter. If you agree to the above understanding, please so indicate by supplying your signature in the space provided on the enclosed copy and return it to me at the above address.

Sincerely,

Henry Hardy
Henry Hardy, President

Consented to and agreed on ___*2/15/98*___.

James C. Jones
James C. Jones, Vice President
American Computer Consulting, Inc.

SIGNATURES

The contract and the letter agreement above, like all properly prepared contracts, have spaces for signatures. Signatures have an almost magical reputation in our society, no doubt a holdover from small children playing pirates and "oaths" signed in blood. And in fact, your signature is a serious matter. It may be evidence that you have agreed to be legally bound to a promise. You should not give it lightly, and you should certainly not give it unintentionally.

A corporation called Seascape Restaurants, Inc., operated a restaurant called the Magic Moment. A Mr. Rosenberg was one third owner and president of Seascape. Mr. Costas contracted to build a new entrance for the restaurant, and Rosenberg signed the contract. Under Rosenberg's signature was typed "Jeff Rosenberg, the Magic Moment." The contract did not refer to Seascape, and Costas knew nothing of Seascape's existence. After a dispute over performance of the contract, Costas sued Rosenberg personally for breach of contract. Rosenberg replied that the corporation, not he, should be liable for the contract, since the corporation owned the restaurant. But the court disagreed. Since the builder had no way of knowing that Seascape was involved, he should be allowed to rely on Rosenberg's signature and Rosenberg's word that he would keep the promises made in the contract. For all Costas knew, Rosenberg and "Magic Moment" were one and the same.

Rosenberg may have thought he was signing the corporation's signature, but in fact he was signing his own. How can you tell the difference? The following forms are examples of various types of signatures. If you are signing a contract on behalf of a corporation or some other entity besides yourself, you must be certain that the context is clear or else risk Mr. Rosenberg's fate. Don't just put your signature on a line because it is there. Make sure the document fits the situation; don't try to make the signature fit the preprinted document.

The law is actually flexible about what constitutes a signature. Whatever you put on a piece of paper intending to be your signature will be sufficient. You can write someone else's name or someone else can write your name, but if you intend it to be your signature, and this intent can be proven in court, then it is your signature. Courts have recognized signatures written in the wrong place on the paper, and various kinds of marks other than names. The question is the intent.

SIGNATURE OF
AN INDIVIDUAL

But the proper method for an individual's signature on a contract is found in Sample Form 3. This is a signature "under seal." In this case, the signer's seal is the word "seal" at the end of the signature line. No rubber stamp or gob of wax is required. In some states, signing a document under seal is of little consequence, and it is rare that a document must be under seal in order to be valid and enforceable (often, however, real estate deeds must be under seal). In some states, seals do have an important consequence. A seal may make it easier to prove the validity of the contract in court or increase the statute of limitations for suing for a breach of the contract. To cover those states or situations where it may be important, the word "seal" will be used in many of the examples in this book.

Sample Form 3. Signature of an individual—

Henry Hardy _____ (Seal)
Henry Hardy

SIGNATURE OF A
SOLE
PROPRIETOR

The signature of a sole proprietorship is really the same as an individual's signature, because the owner of the business operates it as an individual rather than as a separate entity. But if the business is conducted under a trade name (or *fictitious* or *assumed* name) confusion may result. Sample Form 4 makes it clear that the signature is that of a sole proprietor rather than a corporation or some other business organization. The letters "d/b/a" stand for "doing business as." In its place, you may sometimes see "t/a" for "transacting as."

Sample Form 4. Signature of a sole proprietor business—

Henry Hardy   (Seal)

Henry Hardy, a sole proprietor
d/b/a Scrupulous Enterprises

SIGNATURES OF CORPORATIONS

Like individuals, corporations can sign documents under seal or not. The corporate seal usually carries somewhat more meaning than an individual's. In addition to the effects of an individual's seal mentioned above, the corporate seal entitles other parties to the agreement to presume that the signer acted under the appropriate authorization of the corporation's board of directors. Corporate seals are usually rubber stamps or embossers, but anything the corporation's board of directors adopts by resolution as the corporate seal will do. Sample Form 5 shows the signature of a corporation not under seal, and Sample Form 6 that of a corporation under seal. Note that the secretary of the corporation is the custodian of the seal and is responsible for "attesting" that the president or vice president's signature is affixed by the board's authority.

Sample Form 5. Corporate signature (one officer)—

Scrupulous Corporation

By: *Henry Hardy*
Henry Hardy, President

Sample Form 6. Corporate signature (under seal)—

Scrupulous Corporation

By: *Henry Hardy*
Henry Hardy, President

Attest: *Calvin Collier*
Calvin Collier, Secretary

SIGNATURES OF
GENERAL
PARTNERSHIPS

It may be helpful to think of a partnership as a group of sole proprietors in business together, where each member of the group acts as the agent of all the others. It is fundamental to partnership law that each partner is bound by the acts of the others in furtherance of the business and that each partner is liable for the debts of the partnership. It used to be that the law refused to recognize the partnership as an entity separate from the partners. This meant, for example, that a real estate deed for partnership property had to be signed by all of the partners.

The modern rule, which is followed by the Uniform Partnership Act, the Revised Uniform Partnership Act (one of these have been enacted in all states except Louisiana), and the Louisiana Partnership Act, recognizes the separate existence of the partnership and holds that one partner, acting within his or her authority, can bind the rest of the partners on most contracts including deeds. This does not solve all the problems. Many states do not require general partnerships to publish lists of partners or explanations of the limits of their authority. It's not always possible to tell who is a partner or what limits there may be on a signer's authority. For this reason, persons entering into agreements with general partners should take precautions to make sure that the person signing has adequate authority. Sometimes all the partners will be asked to sign a document even though it may not be strictly required by the law to make a contract enforceable. You should have a written partnership agreement. A very simple agreement is provided as Form 19 in the appendix.

You may see the initials "LLP" after the name of a partnership. It means that the partnership is a *limited liability partnership* which is not the same as a *limited partnership* described below. A partner in a LLP is not liable for certain damages caused by his or her partner. For example, a lawyer in a law firm organized as a LLP will not be liable for the legal malpractice committed by another partner in the firm unless the malpractice was committed under the supervision of the first lawyer.

Sample Form 7 shows the signature of a partnership, where one of the general partners has signed for the partnership.

Sample Form 7. General partnership signature—

Scrupulous Associates, a general partnership

By: _____*Henry Hardy*_____ (Seal)
Henry Hardy, General Partner

SIGNATURES OF
LIMITED
PARTNERSHIPS

A limited partnership is much like a general partnership except that, in addition to general partners, it has a special category of *limited partners* who do not participate in management of the business and are not liable for the debts and liabilities of the business beyond the amount of their investment or *contribution*. A limited partnership is created under a special state statute, usually the Uniform Limited Partnership Act, and will have the words "limited partnership" as part of its name.

Only a general partner (there may be one or more) will have authority to sign contracts, and limited partners usually have no authority to sign contracts for, or otherwise represent, the limited partnership.

Sample Form 8. Limited partnership signature—

Scrupulous Hardy Enterprises, a limited partnership

By: _____*Henry Hardy*_____ (Seal)
Henry Hardy, General Partner

NOTARIES AND ACKNOWLEDGMENTS

A notary public is empowered by the state to administer various oaths and to testify to the genuineness of signatures. The term *acknowledgment* refers to a signer's statement that he or she truly is that person, intends to sign the document, and that (in the case of a corporate officer) he or she holds the corporate office claimed. The notary will verify the identity of the signer and affirm in writing that the person signing the document is who he or she claims to be.

Sample Form 9. Acknowledgment by an individual—

STATE OF   TEXAS   )
COUNTY OF   HOCKLEY   )

     I certify that _____ Henry Hardy _____ ,who ☒ is personally known to me to be the person whose name is subscribed to the foregoing instrument ❑ produced _____ as identification, personally appeared before me on ___ May 6, 1998 ___ , and ☒ acknowledged the execution of the foregoing instrument ☒ acknowledged that (s)he is (Assistant) Secretary of Scrupulous Corporation _____ and that by authority duly given and as the act of the corporation, the foregoing instrument was signed in its name by its (Vice) President, sealed with its corporate seal and attested by him/her as its (Assistant) Secretary.

_____

Notary Public, State of

My commission expires: Sept., 30, 2000

Sample Form 10. Acknowledgment by a corporation—

STATE OF   TEXAS   )
COUNTY OF   HOCKLEY   )

     I certify that ___ Calvin Collier ___ ,who ❑ is personally known to me to be the person whose name is subscribed to the foregoing instrument ☒ produced ___ Texas Drivers Lic. ___ as identification, personally appeared before me on ___ May 6, 1998 ___ , and ❑ acknowledged the execution of the foregoing instrument ☒ acknowledged that (s)he is (~~Assistant~~) Secretary of Scrupulous Corporation ___ , and that by authority duly given and as the act of the corporation, the foregoing instrument was signed in its name by its (~~Vice~~) President, sealed with its corporate seal and attested by him/~~her~~ as its (~~Assistant~~) Secretary.

_____

Notary Public, State of

My commission expires: Sept., 30, 2000

Amendment of a Contract

Sometimes the parties to a contract will come to the conclusion that it no longer reflects their agreement and needs to be modified. Unless otherwise agreed in the original contract, the modification of a contract is a contract in its own right and must contain all the elements described earlier in this chapter, including consideration. Sample Form 11 is a general form for amending an existing contract. Also see Sample Form 25 which is a form for amending a lease.

Sample Form 11. Amendment of a contract—

Amendment to Contract

For valuable consideration, the receipt and sufficiency of which is acknowledged by each of the parties, this agreement amends a Contract dated ___February 12, 1998___, between ___Scrupulous Corporation of America___ and ___American Computer Consulting, Inc.___, relating to ___computer consulting services___. This contract amendment is hereby incorporated into the Contract.

Paragraph 1 is amended to read as follows:

1. ACC will provide SCA with ten hours of computer consulting services during the period from February 19, 1998 through March 1, 1998.

Except as changed by this amendment, the Contract shall continue in effect according to its terms. The amendments herein shall be effective on the date this document is executed by all parties.

Executed on ___February 21, 1998___.

Scrupulous Corporation of America   American Computer Consulting, Inc.

Henry Hardy

Henry Hardy, President

Calvin Collier

Calvin Collier, Secretary
(Corporate Seal)

James C. Jones

James C. Jones, Vice Pres.

Jackson C. Jones

Jackson C. Jones, Secretary
(Corporate Seal)

ASSIGNMENT OF A CONTRACT

The right to performance under a contract is a property right like any other and ordinarily can be bought and sold. Courts distinguish between the assignment of a right to receive performance from the other party, and the delegation of your duty to perform.

For example, if you are the landlord under an apartment rental agreement, you can assign the right to receive the monthly rent payments to another party, without delegating your duty to maintain the property. If you are the tenant you can delegate your duty to pay rent to a replacement tenant (as well as assign your right to live in the apartment). (See chapter 5.) The difference is that after you assign your rights, you don't have them any more; but after you delegate your duties, you may not be entirely rid of them. If the substitute tenant fails to pay the rent, the landlord will still be able to collect from you. (However, the written terms of the rental agreement may alter these basic legal rules.)

Many people use the term *contract assignment* to mean both the assignment of rights and the delegation of duties. However, if you intend to delegate a duty, it is better to be specific. If you wish to rid yourself of the possibility of ever having to perform the duty, you must be released from that duty by the person entitled to receive the performance (the landlord in the previous example).

An example of a contract assignment may be found on the following page as Sample Form 12.

Sample Form 12. Assignment of a contract—

ASSIGNMENT OF CONTRACT

FOR VALUE RECEIVED the undersigned (the "Assignor") hereby assigns, transfers and conveys to <u>Bartholomew Simpson, d/b/a B.S. Painting</u> (the "Assignee") all the Assignor's rights, title and interests in and to a contract (the "Contract") dated <u>June 3, 1998</u>, between <u>the Assignor</u> and <u>Fred's Appliance Warehouse, Inc.</u>.

The Assignor hereby warrants and represents that the Contract is in full force and effect and is fully assignable.

The Assignee hereby assumes the duties and obligations of the Assignor under the Contract and agrees to hold the Assignor harmless from any claim or demand thereunder.

The date of this assignment is <u>June 8, 1998</u>.

IN WITNESS WHEREOF this assignment is signed by the parties under seal.

Assignor: Assignee:

Acme Painters, Inc.

By: *Robert Sherwyn*   *Bartholomew Simpson* (seal)
Robert Sherwyn, President   Bartholomew Simpson,
                                                     d/b/a B.S. Painting

---

Having assigned a contract, it is important to notify the person expecting to receive the performance that the assignment has been made. Suppose the assigned contract is an agreement to move 100 cases of wine from warehouse A to warehouse B. Quick Moving Co., assigns the moving contract to Fast Movers, Inc., which promptly does the job, but neglects to notify the owner of the wine that the contract has been assigned. The owner arrives at warehouse B, discovers the job complete, and sends a check for the moving job to Quick Moving Co. Fast Movers then asks to be paid. Fast Movers cannot recover its fee from the owner, because the owner has performed his part of the contract, paying for the completed job, as required by the terms of the agreement. Fast Movers will have to hope it can recover the fee from Quick Moving. If Fast Movers had promptly notified the owner of the assignment, then the owner would have paid Fast Movers directly.

Sample Form 13 is an example of the type of letter that may be used to notify someone that the assignee of a contract has assumed the duty to perform some service for the person notified and that payment should therefore be sent to the assignee. Frequently the contract being assigned is the right to receive payment for a debt. See Sample Form 48 in chapter 8 for a notice to the debtor that future payments should be made to the assignee of the debt.

Sample Form 13. Notice of assignment of a contract—

B.S. Painting
8321 S. Main Street, Fort Worth, TX 76011

June 8, 1998

Fred Jackson, President
Fred's Appliance Warehouse, Inc.
842 US Hwy. 81
Fort Worth, TX 76012

Dear Mr. Jackson:

We are pleased to inform you that we have assumed the duties of Acme Painters, Inc., pursuant to a contract dated June 3, 1996, in which Acme Painters, Inc., agreed to paint your building at 842 US Hwy. 81, Fort Worth, Texas.

Any questions you may have, and all payments due from you pursuant to the contract, should be directed to the undersigned at the address given above.

Sincerely,

Bartholomew Simpson

Bartholomew Simpson, d/b/a
B.S. Painting

TERMINATING CONTRACTS

Contracts are terminated for different reasons and under different circumstances. One is that all the parties to a contract have completely performed the duties they had to perform according to its terms. But suppose that, before the parties completely perform their duties, they decide to call it off. Sample Form 14 is the basic language for an agreement between two parties to a terminate a contract and release each other from all duties to be performed.

Sample Form 14. Termination of an agreement by consent of the parties—

Agreement to Terminate Contract

The undersigned have entered into a contract dated <u>June 3, 1998</u> for the purpose of <u>painting a building</u>.
The undersigned acknowledge that, by their mutual agreement, such contract is hereby terminated without further recourse by either party.

This termination agreement is effective on <u>June 12, 1998</u>.

Another way for a contract to be terminated is for one or more parties to breach the agreement so completely that the other parties are relieved of their duties to perform. For example, if you contract to have your house painted and the painter completely fails to perform the job, then you are relieved of your promise to pay.

Most breaches are not so clear-cut of course. Usually if one party believes the other is not living up to its duties, the party in default will be notified of its shortcomings and a period of negotiation and compromise will follow. Sample Form 15 is a notice given by one party to another that the latter is not living up to a promise.

Sample Form 15. Notice of breach—

Notice of Breach

June 12, 1998

To: Bartholomew Simpson, d/b/a B.S. Painting

We refer to a contract dated _____June 3, 1998_____ (the "Contract")
pursuant to which you have obligated yourself to <u>paint our entire building.</u>

You have breached your duties under the Contract in that you have failed to
<u>paint the south wall</u>. We demand that you cure such default promptly. In the
event that you fail to do so within seven days of the date of this letter, we will refer
the matter to attorneys for immediate action.

Sincerely,

Fred Jackson

Fred Jackson, President
Fred's Appliance Warehouse, Inc.

EMPLOYEES 2

This chapter discusses various aspects of having employees. Matters concerning independent contractors are covered in chapter 3. Form 5 in the appendix is an application for employment, which can be used either alone or with an applicant's resumé. The information obtained can be useful in comparing applicants and checking employment history. In hiring employees it is a good idea to develop some kind of ranking criteria so that you can justify your hiring decisions if you are ever confronted with a charge of illegal discrimination by an unsuccessful applicant.

An important matter not to be overlooked is being sure your prospective employee is legally eligible to work in the United States. Form 18 in the appendix is the I-9 Employment Eligibility Form required by the federal government. The form includes instructions.

EMPLOYMENT CONTRACTS

It is not necessary to have a written employment contract, however, contracts for employment that cannot be completed within a year may not be enforceable unless they are in writing. Some businesses have a policy against employment contracts and hire their employees *at will*, meaning that they can be fired or can quit at any time. But often the law limits the conditions under which even an at will employee can be fired.

Sample Form 16, on the following page, is a simple employment contract for a permanent, salaried employee. Sample Forms 17 through 19, on subsequent pages, show how the pertinent sections of the contract would be completed for various other types of employment situations.

Sample Form 16. Employment contract for a salaried employee—

EMPLOYMENT AGREEMENT

This employment agreement is entered into by and between _____
__Leona Halsey_____(the "Employee") and _____
__Southern Hotel Supply, Inc._____ (the "Employer"), who agree as follows:

1. The Employer has hired the Employee to fill the following position:
   Account and Billing Supervisor

   ☒ See attached description.

2. Term. The term of Employee's employment shall begin on _October 7, 1998_. Employment pursuant to this agreement shall be "at will" and may be ended by the Employee or by the Employer at any time and for any reason. This is an agreement for employment that is:

   ☒ permanent, but "at will."

   ☐ temporary, but "at will," _____
   _____.

3. Probation. It is understood that the first ___60___ days of employment shall be probationary only and that if the Employee's services are not satisfactory to the Employer employment shall be terminated at the end of this probationary period.

4. Compensation and Benefits. The Employee's compensation and benefits during the term of this agreement shall be as stated in this paragraph, and may be adjusted from time to time by the Employer. Initially, the Employer shall pay the Employee:

   ☒ a salary in the amount of __$19,240 per year_____,
   payable _at the rate of $370 each week_____.

   ☐ an hourly wage of $_____ , payable _____.

   ☐ a commission of _____% of _____.
   In addition to such commission, the Employee shall receive _____
   _____.

   ☒ the following benefits: _Employer will provide group health insurance_____
   _____after successful completion of probationary period_____.

   ☐ other:

5. Work Hours. The hours and schedule worked by the Employee may be adjusted from time to time by the Employer. Initially, the Employee shall work the following hours each week:

   9:00 a.m. to 5:00 p.m., Monday through Friday.

6. Additional Terms. The Employee also agrees to the terms of the attached:

❑ No other agreements are attached   ☒ Confidentiality Agreement

❑ Agreement on Patents and Inventions   ❑ Indemnification Agreement

❑ Other:_____

7. This agreement shall be governed by the laws of ___Florida_____.

8. It is the Employer's intention to comply with all federal, state and local laws which apply to the business, including but not limited to labor, equal opportunity, privacy and sexual harassment laws. The Employee shall promptly report to the Employer any violations encountered in the business. The Employee shall at all time comply with any and all federal, state and local laws.

9. The Employee shall not have the power to make any contracts or commitments on behalf of the Employer without the express written consent of the Employer.

10. In the event one party fails to insist upon performance of a part of this agreement, such failure shall not be construed as waiving those terms, and this entire agreement shall remain in full force.

11. In the event a dispute of any nature arises between the parties to this agreement, the parties agree to submit the dispute to binding arbitration under the rules of the American Arbitration Association. An award rendered by the arbitrator(s) shall be final and binding upon the parties and judgment on such award may be entered by either party in the highest court having jurisdiction. Each party specifically waives his or her right to bring the dispute before a court of law and stipulates that this agreement shall be a complete defense to any action instituted in any local, state or federal court or before any administrative tribunal.

12. If any part of this agreement is adjudged invalid, illegal, or unenforceable, the remaining parts shall not be affected and shall remain in full force and effect.

13. This agreement shall be binding upon the parties, and upon their heirs, executors, personal representatives, administrators, and assigns. No person shall have a right or cause of action arising out of or resulting from this agreement except those who are parties to it and their successors in interest.

14. This is instrument, including any attached agreements specified in paragraph 5 above, constitutes the entire agreement of the parties. No representations or promises have been made except those that are set out in this agreement. This agreement may not be modified except in writing signed by all the parties.

15. This agreement was executed by the parties on ___October 7, 1998_____.

Employer:
Southern Hotel Supply, Inc.

Employee:

By *Jake Southern*_____

Jake Southern, President

*Leona Halsey*_____(Seal)

Leona Halsey

Sample Form 17. Employment contract for a commissioned employee—

4. Compensation and Benefits. The Employee's compensation and benefits during the term of this agreement shall be as stated in this paragraph, and may be adjusted from time to time by the Employer. Initially, the Employer shall pay the Employee:

❑ a salary in the amount of _____,
   payable _____.

❑ an hourly wage of $_____ , payable _____.

☒ a commission of __5__ % of _____ gross sales receipts _____.
   In addition to such commission, the Employee shall receive _____
   _____ an expense account of $100 per week _____.

☒ the following benefits: group medical and dental insurance coverage _____
   _____.

❑ other:

Sample Form 18. Employment contract for part-time employee (hourly wage)—

5. Work Hours. The hours and schedule worked by the Employee may be adjusted from time to time by the Employer. Initially, the Employee shall work the following hours each week:

8:00 a.m. to 12:30 p.m., on Mondays, Wednesdays, and Fridays.

Sample Form 19. Employment contract for temporary employee—

2. Term. The term of Employee's employment shall begin on _____ October 7, 1998 _____.
Employment pursuant to this agreement shall be "at will" and may be ended by the Employee or by the Employer at any time and for any reason. This is an agreement for employment that is:

❑ permanent, but "at will."

☒ temporary, but "at will," for the period of October 7, 1998, to
   January 4, 1999, at such times and on such dates as needed .

THE OFFICER AS EMPLOYEE

An officer is always an agent of the corporation, but it is not always true that an officer is an employee of the corporation. For example, an officer may be the employee of a parent corporation who serves as an officer of a subsidiary as a convenience to the employer parent. Or the corporation may be a small family company where a spouse serves as secretary or assistant secretary as a convenience to the person who runs the business.

Where the officer is an employee, it may be desirable to have a written employment contract. (For a comprehensive treatment of corporations, including corporate officer employment forms, see Forms 10.06-10.10 in *The Most Valuable Corporate Forms You'll Ever Need*, by James C. Ray, available from your local bookstore or directly from Sourcebooks, Inc., by calling 1-800-226-5291. That book also contains resolutions for adoption by a corporate board of directors authorizing employment contracts and setting salaries for employees.)

RESIGNATION AND TERMINATION

At will employees serve at the pleasure of the employer, subject to certain state and federal regulations. An employment agreement may be for a specific term, but that doesn't mean the employer must keep an employee it doesn't want. However, depending on the employment contract, the employer could be liable for damages to the employee as a result of such termination. Similarly, an employee with such a contract could resign at any time, but if the resignation is in breach of the agreement, the employee could be liable for damages. An employee's resignation can be as simple as a letter addressed to the employer (possibly to the employee's supervisor or the person who hired him or her) stating something like: "I hereby resign my employment as packaging manager, effective March 31, 1998, at 5:00 p.m." It should be dated, and signed by the employee. To make it final and irreversible, it is a good idea to give the employee a letter accepting his or her resignation.

SPECIAL EMPLOYMENT AGREEMENTS

CONFIDENTIALITY

Often an employee will learn information about the business that the employer wants kept secret. A confidentiality agreement (Form 7 in the appendix) creates a contractual obligation to keep the secret. If the secret is revealed, the employee will be liable to the employer for damages resulting from the breach. In the case of trade secrets and other important matters, the damages the employee is capable of paying may be far less than the actual damages incurred, so it is best not to rely too much on such an agreement. Give employees information on a "need to know" basis if possible, and hire employees you can trust. Ideally, a confidentiality agreement should be made a part of the employment agreement. Often an employer won't think of the need for a confidentiality agreement until after an employee is hired. This oversight leads to a common mistake: failure to include the contract element of consideration paid by the employer in exchange for the employee's promise of confidentiality. Promising to continue the employee's employment (a right he or she may already have) may not be enough. Form 7 in the appendix allows for additional consideration such as cash, a raise in salary, or an extension of the term of employment.

PATENTS,
INVENTIONS,
COPYRIGHTS,
ETC.

Another fruitful area for disputes is where an employee creates a patentable invention, or copyrightable material. The question becomes: who owns it, the employer or the employee? Without a specific agreement, a court may have to decide, considering such matters as the employee's job description, the nature of the invention or material, and whether it was created on company time and using company resources. Form 8 in the appendix is an agreement on patents and inventions designed to provide protection for the employer. Forms 12, 14, and 15 can be used for either an employee or a non-employee to commission an artist or author to create a specific work for you, with you obtaining all rights to the work (Form 12); for you to acquire the copyrights in an existing work (Form 14); or where the owner of a copyright is willing to authorize you to use his or her copyrighted work for certain purposes, but is not willing to give up all rights (Form 15).

INDEMNIFICATION

Employees may be reluctant to work in certain capacities (especially as corporate officers) if there is a danger they may get sued. It may help to offer the employee an indemnification agreement (Form 11 in the appendix). This is simply an agreement whereby the employer agrees to pay for any consequences of a lawsuit against the employee.

NON-
COMPETITION
AGREEMENTS

You may want to be sure that an employee doesn't learn your business, then quit to open his or her own business and compete with you. This can be prevented by having the employee sign a non-competition agreement (Form 9 in the appendix). Such an agreement typically prohibits the employee from competing within a certain geographical area and for a certain period of time (provided the restrictions are reasonable).

REFERENCES

There was a time when employers treated references for former employees lightly. Glowing references were given routinely, and if they were less than glowing, so be it. No more. If a former employee's prospective new employer asks you for a reference, and you mislead him or her, you could conceivably be liable for damages to the new employer caused by hiring a bad employee. Suppose for example, you know your former employee had stolen from the company, but you don't mention it in a letter of recommendation. The employee later steals quite a lot from the new employer. Will you be liable for not mentioning the history of theft? There may also be liability from the other direction. Suppose you say something less than flattering about a former employee and it turns out to be untrue (or you just can't prove it). Will you be liable for defamation? Many employers now refuse to give references and will only confirm dates of employment and salary history. Sample Form 20 is a response to a request for references that provides only limited information.

Sample Form 20. Response to inquiry regarding former employee—

Scrupulous Corporation of America ————————————
400 West 61st Avenue, P.O. Box 19, New York, NY 10032

February 12, 1998

George Dempsey, Personnel Director
Kent, Goldsmith & Fargo, P.A.
2473 Washington St., Suite 2300
Philadelphia, PA 10607

Dear Mr. Dempsey:

We have received your request for a reference regarding a former employee of this company. It is our policy not to provide such references or disclose reasons for termination. However, we are able to confirm that Jean Walker was employed by us from March 1, 1988 through September 12, 1997. Her ending rate of pay was $18,000 per year.

No conclusion adverse to our former employee should be drawn from this response. Our policy with regard to references does not imply any dissatisfaction with the performance or conduct of any former employee.

Sincerely,

Carl Franklin

Carl Franklin,
Personnel Director

INDEPENDENT CONTRACTORS 3

EMPLOYEE OR INDEPENDENT CONTRACTOR?

It's an important distinction. An employer owes significant legal duties to an employee that it may not owe to an independent contractor. Perhaps even more important, an employer owes duties to the government on account of an employee such as taxes, workers' compensation, and the like. An employer may be liable to a third party for the negligence of an employee where it would not be liable for the negligence of an independent contractor.

And it's not always easy to tell which is which. Just because you and someone you hire explicitly agree between yourselves at the time of the hire that it will be an independent contractor relationship, that doesn't mean a court or the IRS will agree with you if the issue comes up later.

There's a list of factors to be considered. A "yes" answer to all or most of the following questions will likely mean that the person hired is an independent contractor rather than an employee (for more information and certainty, get IRS Form SS-8):

1. Does the person hired exercise independent control over the details of the work such as the methods used to complete the job?

2. Is the person hired in a business different from that of the person hiring? (For example, where a plumber is hired by a lawyer.)

3. Does the person hired work as a specialist without supervision by the person hiring?

4. Does the person hired supply his or her own tools?

5. Is the person hired for only a short period of time rather than consistently over a relatively long period?

6. Does the job require a relatively high degree of skill?

7. Is the person paid "by the job" rather than "by the hour"?

INDEPENDENT
CONTRACTORS

Contracts with independent contractors don't have to be in writing, but it's often even more important that they are writing than that an employment agreement is. For one thing, the writing is an opportunity to state clearly that you intend it to be an independent contractor arrangement. Also, since by definition you have relatively little control over the way an independent contractor does the work, the writing may be your last chance to influence important matters like exactly what the job is and when it must be completed. It's often tempting to use the word "employer" in these contracts, however, it is not appropriate since the independent contractor is not "employed" (and you don't want the IRS thinking otherwise). Sample Forms 21 and 22, on the following pages, are two examples of independent contractor agreements.

Sample Form 21. Appointment of independent sales representative (payment by commission)—

APPOINTMENT OF SALES REPRESENTATIVE

This agreement is entered into by between ____Howard Parsons____ (the "Agent") and __Scrupulous Corporation__ (the "Company"). It is agreed by the Agent and the Company as follows:

1.   The Company has appointed the Agent as its representative for the sale of __products__ in the following territory: __Alabama, Florida, Georgia and Mississippi__. The territory may be changed from time to time upon agreement by the Company and the Agent. The Agent agrees to use his or her best efforts in the sale of such in the territory assigned.

2.   The term of Agent's appointment shall begin on ____January 1, 1998____. Appointment pursuant to this agreement may be ended by the Agent or by the Company at any time and for any reason.

3.   All sales made by the Agent shall be at prices and terms set from time to time by the Company, and no contracts for sale shall be valid until accepted by a duly authorized officer of the Company.

4.   The Agent's compensation and benefits during the term of this agreement shall be as stated in this paragraph, and may be adjusted from time to time by the Company. The Company shall pay the Agent a commission of ____10____% based on the net selling price of the goods actually received by the Company. In the event part or all of the purchase price is refunded to the purchaser for any reason, the Agent's commission based on such amounts refunded shall be returned by the Agent to the Company or deducted by the Company from the Agent's future commissions. The Company shall not be liable to the Agent for commissions on orders unfilled by the Company for any reason. In addition to the commissions provided for in this agreement, the Agent shall receive __$100/wk. expense account__.

5.   The Company shall reimburse the Agent for expenses according to a schedule published from time to time by the Corporation.

6.   The parties agree that no employer - employee relationship is created by this agreement, but that the relationship of the Agent to the Company shall be that of an independent contractor.

This agreement was executed by the Agent and by the Company on __December 22, 1997__.

Company: Scrupulous Corporation   Agent:

By: *Henry Hardy*   *Howard Parsons*
_____   _____(Seal)
Henry Hardy, President   Howard Parsons

Sample Form 22. Independent contractor agreement—

INDEPENDENT CONTRACTOR AGREEMENT

This agreement is entered into by and between <u>Stainproof Carpets, Inc.</u>
_____ (the "Company") and <u>Joe King</u>
_____ (the "Contractor"). It is agreed by the parties
as follows:

1. The Contractor shall supply all of the labor and materials to perform the following work for the Company as an independent contractor:

Installation of carpet and pad in five residences listed
in paragraph 2 below; carpet and pad to be provided by the
Company.

❑ The attached plans and specifications are to be followed and are hereby made a
part of this Agreement.

2. The Contractor agrees to the following completion dates for portions of the
work and final completion of the work:

Description of Work	Completion Date
1492 Columbus Dr.	October 4, 1998
1776 S. Washington Blvd.	October 5, 1998
1066 Normandy Lane	October 6, 1998
1929 Wall Street	October 7, 1998
1215 Magna Carta Cir.	October 9, 1998

3. The Contractor shall perform the work in a workman-like manner, according to
standard industry practices, unless other standards or requirements are set forth in any
attached plans and specifications.

4. The Company shall pay the Contractor the sum of $<u>$1,750.00</u>, in
full payment for the work as set forth in this Agreement, to be paid as follows:

5. Any additional work or services shall be agreed to in writing, signed by both parties.

---

6. The Contractor shall obtain and maintain any licenses or permits necessary for the work to be performed. The Contractor shall obtain and maintain any required insurance, including but not limited to workers' compensation insurance, to cover the Contractor's employees and agents.

7. The Contractor shall be responsible for the payment of any sub-contractors and shall obtain lien releases from sub-contractors as may be necessary. The Contractor agrees to indemnify and hold harmless the Company from any claims or liability arising out of the work performed by the Contractor under this Agreement.

8. Time is of the essence of this Agreement.

9. This instrument, including any attached exhibits and addenda, constitutes the entire agreement of the parties. No representations or promises have been made except those that are set out in this agreement. This agreement may not be modified except in writing signed by all the parties.

10. This agreement shall be governed by the laws of ___North Carolina___.

This agreement was executed by the parties on ___September 30, 1998___.

Company: Stainproof Carpet, Inc.   Contractor: Joe King

George T. Berber   *Joe King*_____(Seal)
George T. Berber, President   Joe King

Attest: *Margaret G. Saxony*
Margaret G. Saxony, Secretary

(Corporate Seal)

CONSULTANTS

Consultants are a category of independent contractors. Frequently they are hired without any sort of written agreement, but it's hard to imagine a situation in which a written agreement is not better. Many consultants will have their own standard form agreements for you to sign.

ACCOUNTANTS

Accountants provide a variety of services, from "bookkeeping" and preparation of tax forms, to the formal "audit" of a company's financial statements. Audits are expensive and, for most corporations, not necessary. An audit may be required by some regulatory agency or by contract with some institution. Be careful that you don't lightly sign an agreement with a lender or some other party that requires the production of "audited financial statements." You may be getting into more than you bargained for.

LAWYERS

Lawyers are predictably creative about the ways in which you can pay them. Usually contracts for legal services provide for payment by the hour, by the task, or, where the client is a plaintiff in a law suit asking for money damages, on a contingent basis. A contingent fee is an arrangement in which the lawyer gets a share of the client's recovery, whatever that may be. Always insist on a written fee agreement with a lawyer.

Powers of Attorney 4

A *power of attorney* is a written authority for someone to act as your agent. The agent is often called an *attorney in fact*. (This has no relationship to an *attorney at law*.) Corporations don't ordinarily execute powers of attorney, because corporate officers are already the appointed agents of the company. If you want the vice president to perform some task on behalf of the company, you can simply have the board of directors authorize the act in a resolution. However, on some occasions it may be appropriate to use a power of attorney to authorize an officer, director, employee, or other person to perform a certain act.

A power of attorney can be for a particular duty and expire when that duty is done (see Sample Form 23, or it can authorize a wide range of activity and last for an indefinite period of time (see Form 21 in the appendix). A power of attorney can usually be revoked at any time by the person giving it (who is called the *grantor*). Ordinarily, powers of attorney may be canceled at any time by the grantor. Sample Form 24 is a form for that purpose. Of course the attorney in fact may resign an appointment at any time.

If the grantor were a corporation, the power of attorney would be signed by the president or vice president, and attested by the secretary or assistant secretary. The notary would then notarize the secretary's signature. See chapter 1 for more information about signatures and notary acknowledgments.

Sample Form 23. Simple power of attorney for a particular purpose—

LIMITED POWER OF ATTORNEY

Scrupulous Enterprises _____ (the "Grantor") hereby grants to James Bond _____ (the "Agent") a limited power of attorney. As the Grantor's attorney in fact, the Agent shall have full power and authority to undertake and perform the following on behalf of the Grantor: Execute a contract and financing documents for the purchase and financing of a 1999 Chevrolet Astro delivery van.

By accepting this grant, the Agent agrees to act in a fiduciary capacity consistent with the reasonable best interests of the Grantor. This power of attorney may be revoked by the Grantor at any time; however, any person dealing with the Agent as attorney in fact may rely on this appointment until receipt of actual notice of termination.

IN WITNESS WHEREOF, the undersigned grantor has executed this power of attorney under seal as of the date stated above.

Scrupulous Enterprises,
a general partnership

Attest: (Not applicable)_____   *Henry Hardy*_____(Seal)
                              Secretary   Grantor

STATE OF   NEW YORK
COUNTY OF   JAMAICA

I certify that Henry Hardy_____ ,who ☒ is personally known to me to be the person whose name is subscribed to the foregoing instrument ❏ produced _____ as identification, personally appeared before me on May 10, 1998_____, and ❏ acknowledged the execution of the foregoing instrument ❏ acknowledged that (s)he is (Assistant) Secretary of _____ and that by authority duly given and as the act of the corporation, the foregoing instrument was signed in its name by its (Vice) President, sealed with its corporate seal and attested by him/her as its Secretary.

*Penny Moneypenny*_____
Notary Public, State of New York
Notary's commission expires: Oct. 31, 2000

I hereby accept the foregoing appointment as attorney in fact on May 10, 1998_____.

*James Bond*_____ Attorney in Fact

Sample Form 24. Cancellation of power of attorney—

REVOCATION OF POWER OF ATTORNEY

The appointment of James Bond as the attorney in fact of the undersigned Grantor (the "Grantor") made on May 10, 1998, is hereby revoked and terminated by the Grantor effective on this date.

Signed on April 1, 1998.

Scrupulous Enterprises, a general partnership

*Henry Hardy*_____(Seal)
Henry Hardy, general partner, Grantor

Buying, Selling, and Leasing Real Estate

5

Buying and Selling Real Estate

Unless your business is the purchase, development and resale of real property, it is likely that the decision to buy or sell land or buildings represents a significant step. It will follow careful and possibly quite lengthy consideration, including a period of investigation, appraisal and thought about the future of your business. If your business is a corporation or some form of partnership, the issue may be visited several times by the board of directors or partners who may want to be involved at every step. (See *The Most Valuable Corporate Forms You'll Ever Need* for minutes of directors' meetings considering the purchase of real property.)

Buying and selling real estate has been going on for thousands of years. One of the reasons we human beings developed law in the first place was to protect the ownership of real estate without the need for armed combat. So the laws are hoary and, like the lands they deal with, are uniquely tied to and vary with the jurisdiction. Therefore, this chapter will discuss certain matters to be considered in dealing with real estate and explain the type of forms commonly used, but it will not contain many forms you can use. If you are purchasing or selling commercial real estate, you should consult a real estate attorney. A lawyer who knows the applicable state law and even the recording customs at the local court house will be indispensable even for small real estate transactions. He or she will know what to do about title searches, insurance and countless little details that will loom large if not handled correctly. A real estate purchase is a major step for your business, one that is too important to venture into without professional advice. That said, we will now discuss some of the more common forms you will encounter.

Real estate forms specific for your state can usually be obtained from a real estate sales office (for sales contracts and options) or an office supply store (for deeds).

OPTIONS TO PURCHASE

An *option* is a kind of contract within a contract. It is an agreement to keep an offer "open" for a period of time in exchange for some consideration such as money. As always in a contract, the consideration part is important. It must be real and not just a formal recital or else you might find that you don't have an option at all. Options may be recorded just as deeds. Recording will protect the party with the option from subsequent claims, but it may also trigger a "due on sale" clause in an existing mortgage.

CONTRACT FOR PURCHASE AND SALE

A contract for purchase and sale is usually the first formal step toward a purchase. It is a formal contract that spells out the terms under which the seller agrees to sell and the buyer agrees to buy. Typically such a contract will be elaborate, especially if, for example, it concerns a complex structure occupied by existing tenants and subject to existing mortgages.

It would be unwise to attempt to provide a usable contract for purchase and sale of real estate in this book, when entire books are devoted to this single type of document. For more detailed information on real estate contracts, see the book *How to Negotiate Real Estate Contracts*, by Mark Warda, available at your local bookstore or directly from the publisher, Sourcebooks, Inc. (1-800-226-5291).

DEEDS

A *deed* is a document which formally transfers title, or ownership, of property. There are several types of deeds in regular use. In most cases, you probably need a *warranty deed* in which the seller guarantees, among other things, that the seller has good title to the property, and that, after selling it the buyer will have good title. What makes a warranty deed special is language such as the following:

> To have and to hold such property together with all rights and appurtenances thereto belonging. The grantor is seized of the premises in fee simple and has the right to convey the same in fee simple clear of all encumbrances, and the grantor hereby covenants to warrant and forever defend title to the property against the lawful claims of all persons whomsoever except for the exceptions above stated.

An alternative deed, and the type you would prefer to use if you are the seller, is the *quitclaim deed* which merely says that the seller sells to the buyer whatever the seller owns, if anything, with no guarantees. Quitclaim deeds have their uses, but you probably wouldn't buy property relying on a quitclaim deed alone, and it is unlikely that a knowledgeable person would accept one from you. These days most deeds are fill-in-the-blank forms, each state has its own preferred format, and some states have required formats.

Transfers of real property are usually made under seal and acknowledged. They are "within the Statute of Frauds" and must be in writing (see chapter 1). Since real property can't be literally handed over to the buyer, recording of deeds is critical. It is the way you prove your ownership and the way you prevent someone else from purporting to sell the property that belongs to you.

SIGNATURES

As always, the signatures on options, contracts for purchase and sale, and deeds must be appropriate for the situation, depending upon whether the property owner is an individual, married couple, partnership, corporation, etc. (See the section on signatures in chapter 1.)

CLOSING THE SALE

A real estate closing can be a monumental paper shuffle, especially if the property is complex commercial property. Once again, the value of an attorney experienced in the procedure will be indispensable. But you have a part, too. Keep an eye on the detail. Before the closing, become as familiar as you can with the documents that will pass under your nose. You will know what's important to you better than your lawyer can. There won't be much time for reading and explanations at the closing, and what time there is will likely be charged to you by the hour.

SECURING PAYMENT

Real estate is commonly used to secure payment of a debt, either in connection with the purchase of real property, or to secure a loan unconnected with a real estate purchase. This is done with a *mortgage*, although some states use a document called a *deed of trust*. A mortgage or deed of trust will describe the real estate, refer to the promissory note it secures, and have numerous provisions relating to what happens if the promissory note goes into default. If your property is being mortgaged, the lender on the promissory note will probably prepare the mortgage documents. If you are going to take a mortgage to secure money someone owes to you, you will need to prepare the documents. Since the form for a mortgage, and the requirements for its execution and recording, vary from state to state, no useful form can be provided in a book like this. Mortgage forms can usually be obtained from an office supply store, or possibly from a real estate agent or bank or mortgage company. If you hold a mortgage, you may want to sell it to another party. To do so, you will need to execute an ASSIGNMENT OF MORTGAGE, like Form 25 in the appendix. If you hold the mortgage until it is paid off, you will need to execute a SATISFACTION OF MORTGAGE, like Form 26 in the appendix.

LEASING REAL ESTATE

Leasing real property is a lot like buying it. In fact you are buying it for a period of time, so the process is in some ways similar. A lease or rental agreement is the document that effects the right to temporary possession of real estate. Although it transfers an interest in real estate, as does a deed, a lease is a very different animal. Deeds are usually quite short. Leases are usually quite long. Deeds look very much alike, while leases vary tremendously depending upon the type and function of the property being leased. Residential leases are different from commercial leases.

Some states have required clauses, relating to such matters as security deposits, lead-based paints, and radon testing. The failure to include one of these required clauses could render the lease unenforceable or create some kind of penalty for the landlord. As with buying and selling real estate, you should consult a real estate attorney before signing a lease.

Especially in a long-term commercial lease, or one with renewal options, a lot of money can be at stake. For more detailed information about leases, see the book *How to Negotiate Real Estate Leases*, by Mark Warda, published by Sourcebooks, Inc.

MANAGING THE LEASE

Unlike the sale and purchase of real estate where, after the closing, there is ordinarily little reason for the buyer to be in contact with the seller, a lease is an ongoing relationship. It may require attention or changing from time to time. It may have to be terminated. Following are documents designed to take care of some of the problems that may come up.

AMENDMENTS   Amendments to a lease come in many forms. Sometimes they are called *riders* or *addenda*, but whatever the name, the purpose is to make a change in the standard terms of a lease or terms which have already been agreed upon. Before you sign an amendment, read the provision of the basic lease which says how and under what conditions the lease may be amended. Make sure the amendment you sign conforms to those conditions.

Sample Form 25. Amendment to lease—

AMENDMENT TO LEASE AGREEMENT

For valuable consideration, the receipt and sufficiency of which is hereby acknowledged by each of the parties, this agreement amends a lease agreement (the "Lease") between <u>Stripmall Rentals, Inc.</u> (the "Landlord") and <u>Scrupulous Associates, a general partnership</u> (the "Tenant") dated_____, relating to property located at <u>16249 W. 24th Street, Unit 6, Austin, Texas</u>. This agreement is hereby incorporated into the Lease.

    1. Paragraph 5 of the Lease is hereby amended to read in its entirety as follows:

> 5. Assignment. The Tenant shall not assign this Agreement or sublet the Premises in whole or in part without the written consent of the Landlord.

    2. Paragraph 20.3 of the Lease is hereby deleted in its entirety.

    3. There is hereby added to the Lease a new paragraph number 9.4 which shall read in its entirety as follows:

> 9.4. Provide the Tenant with 10 designated and sign-posted parking spaces in the center parking lot.

    4. Except as changed by this amendment, the Lease shall continue in effect according to its terms. The amendments herein shall be effective on the date this document is executed by both parties.

    Executed on <u>September 7, 1998</u>.

Landlord: StripMall Rentals, Inc.   Tenant: Scrupulous Associates

By: *Albert Smith*   By: *Henry Hardy* (Seal)
    Albert Smith, President   Henry Hardy, General Partner

ASSIGNMENTS
AND SUBLETS

Chapter 1 discussed the assignment of contracts. From the tenant's point of view, assigning a lease means moving out and finding a new tenant. When a landlord assigns a lease it is usually called *assigning rents*, a topic also mentioned in chapter 1.

Assignments and sublets are different. In an assignment, the new tenant steps into the shoes of the old tenant and deals with the landlord directly. If all goes well, the old tenant is out of the picture. Remember that, while a tenant can assign his or her right to use the property, he or she can only delegate the duty to pay rent. This means that, absent an agreement by the landlord, the tenant always remains ultimately responsible for payment of the rent if the lease assignee fails to do so. (The assignment form below provides an optional provision in which the landlord discharges the old tenant from further obligations under the lease. In the example, the partnership tenant has incorporated, and the lease is being assigned to the corporation.)

In a sublease, the old tenant stands between the landlord and the subtenant. In essence, the tenant becomes the landlord to the subtenant. The subtenant will pay rent to the old tenant who will then pay rent to the landlord. The subtenant may pay more rent to the tenant than the tenant will pay to landlord, leaving the tenant a profit. A sublease is actually a special type of lease, and is just as complex as a lease. The failure to include certain provisions required by a state or local law can invalidate a sublease, therefore you should consult an attorney or a book specifically about leases before preparing or signing one. Because of the variety of state and local leasing laws, it is not practical to provide a sublease form in this book.

Almost every written lease agreement will require the landlord's permission before the tenant can validly assign the lease or sublet the premises. Examples of an assignment and a consent to sublease follow. Sample Form 26 makes the landlord a party giving consent to an assignment. As stated earlier, an assignment may or may not release the original tenant from further liability to the landlord, so be sure to note the optional language for paragraph 4 in the example.

Sample Form 26. Lease assignment—

LEASE ASSIGNMENT

This Lease Assignment is entered into by and among <u>Scrupulous Associates</u> _____(the "Assignor"), <u>Scrupulous Corporation</u> (the "Assignee"), and <u>Peachtree Properties, Inc.</u> (the "Landlord"). For valuable consideration, it is agreed by the parties as follows:

1. The Landlord and the Assignor have entered into a lease agreement (the "Lease") dated <u>April 1, 1998</u> concerning the premises described as:

1264 Main Street, #24, Decatur, Georgia.

2. The Assignor hereby assigns, transfers and delivers to the Assignee all of Assignor's rights and delegates all of Assignor's duties under the Lease effective on <u>October 1, 1998</u> (the "Effective Date").

3. The Assignee hereby accepts such assignment of rights and delegation of duties and agrees to pay all rents promptly when due and perform all of Assignor's obligations under the Lease accruing on and after the Effective Date. The Assignee further agrees to indemnify and hold the Assignor harmless from any breach of Assignee's duties hereunder.

4. ☐ The Assignor agrees to transfer possession of the leased premises to the Assignee on the Effective Date. All rents and obligations of the Assignor under the Lease accruing before the Effective Date shall have been paid or discharged as of the Effective Date.

☒ The Landlord hereby assents to the assignment of the Lease hereunder and as of the Effective Date hereby releases and discharges the Assignor from all duties and obligations under the Lease accruing after the Effective Date.

☐ The Landlord hereby assents to the assignment of the Lease hereunder provided that Landlord's assent hereunder shall not discharge the Assignor of its obligations under the Lease in the event of breach by the Assignee. The Landlord will give notice to the Assignor of any such breach by the Assignee, and, provided the Assignor pays all accrued rents and cures any other default of the Assignee, the Assignor may enforce the terms of the Lease and this Assignment against the Assignee, in the name of the Landlord, if necessary.

5. There shall be no further assignment of the Lease without the written consent of the Landlord.

6. This agreement shall be binding upon and inure to the benefit of the parties, their successors, assigns and personal representatives.

This assignment was executed under seal on ___September 27, 1998___ .

Assignor: Scrupulous Associates,   Assignee: Scrupulous Corporation
        a general partnership

By *Henry Hardy* _____   By ___ *Henry Hardy* _____
Henry Hardy, General Partner   Henry Hardy, President

_____   Attest: *Calvin Collier* _____
                                      Calvin Collier, Secretary
Landlord: Peachtree Properties, Inc.

By ___ *Leigh Jackson* _____
Leigh Jackson, President

Attest: *Susan Murphy* _____
Susan Murphy, Secretary

Sample Form 27. Landlord's consent to sublease—

LANDLORD'S CONSENT TO SUBLEASE

FOR VALUABLE CONSIDERATION, the undersigned (the "Landlord") hereby consents to the sublease of all or part of the premises located at ___1264 Main Street, #24, Decatur, Georgia___ , which is the subject of a lease agreement between Landlord and ___Scrupulous Associates___ (the "Tenant"), pursuant to an Agreement to Sublease dated ___April 1, 1998___ , between the Tenant and ___Scrupulous Corporation___ as Subtenant dated ___September 26, 1998___ .

This consent was signed by the Landlord on ___September 28, 1998___ .

                              Landlord: Peachtree Properties, Inc.

                              By: *Leigh Jackson* _____
                              Leigh Jackson, President

EXTENDING OR
RENEWING A
LEASE

Almost any lease will have a provision stating the terms under which it may be extended or renewed. Sometimes advance notice of intent to renew (or to not renew) is required. It is important to read such provisions and comply with them exactly.

Sample Form 28. Notice of intent to renew or extend lease—

Scrupulous Corporation
201 Wacker Drive, Suite 622, Chicago, IL 60602

November 23, 1998

201 Wacker Drive, Inc.
201 Wacker Drive, Suite 1012
Chicago, IL 60602

Dear Sir or Madam:

    Pursuant to paragraph (3) of the Lease Agreement between you as Landlord and the undersigned as Tenant dated December 23, 1997, related to the premises located at 201 Wacker Drive, Suite 622, notice is hereby given of our intent to renew such lease for an additional term of two years.

                    Very truly yours,

TERMINATING A
LEASE

Here we are discussing the termination of a lease at the end of some appropriate term—not termination in mid-term for violation of the terms of the lease. Some leases provide for the termination of the lease upon the occurrence of some event or the passage of a certain amount of time. Some leases operate on a "month to month" basis and continue in effect until notice of termination is given by the landlord or tenant. Either the lease or State law may require a written notice of termination. Failure to give written notice within a required time-frame may result in automatic renewal of the lease. Again, it is important to read your lease and comply exactly with whatever termination provisions it contains, and to know your State's landlord/tenant laws. These laws may also be different for residential and commercial leases. Below is an example of a termination notice given by the tenant, but a slight rearrangement of the words would make it work for a landlord giving notice to a tenant.

Sample Form 29. Notice of termination of lease—

Scrupulous Corporation
201 Wacker Drive, Suite 622, Chicago, IL 60602

November 23, 1998

201 Wacker Drive, Inc.
201 Wacker Drive, Suite 1012
Chicago, IL 60602

Dear Sir or Madam:

Pursuant to paragraph (6) of the Lease Agreement between you as Landlord and the undersigned as Tenant dated December 23, 1997, related to the premises located at 201 Wacker Drive, Suite 622, notice is hereby given that such lease agreement is terminated effective December 31, 1998.

Very truly yours,

Occasionally the landlord and tenant, for whatever reason, will decide to call it quits. Leases, like any contract can be terminated upon the mutual agreement of the parties. Sample Form 30, on the following page, is a mutual agreement to terminate an existing lease. (Also see the topic "Terminating Contracts" in chapter 1.)

Sample Form 30. Agreement to terminate lease—

AGREEMENT TO TERMINATE LEASE

The undersigned have entered into a lease agreement dated December 23, 1997, related to the premises known as 201 Wacker Drive, Suite 622 (the "Lease"). The undersigned acknowledge that, for valuable consideration and by their mutual agreement, effective on November 30, 1998, such Lease is hereby terminated and all rights and obligations of either party shall be canceled except for any obligations under the Lease accrued before the effective termination date.

This termination agreement shall be binding upon the parties, their successors, assigns and personal representatives.

This termination agreement was signed on November 15, 1998.

Landlord: 201 Wacker Drive, Inc.   Tenant: Scrupulous Corporation

By _*Robert Johnson*_   By _*Henry Hardy*_
Robert Johnson, President   Henry Hardy, President

Attest: _*William R. Smith*_   Attest: _*Calvin Collier*_
William R. Smith, Secretary   Calvin Collier, Secretary
(Corporate Seal)   (Corporate Seal)

Compliance with lease terms. Both parties to a lease have a variety of duties. The tenant mostly is required to pay money from time to time, but may also have repair and maintenance duties. The landlord will have some repair duties as well. The following form is an example of the main body of a demand letter.

Sample Form 31. Demand for compliance with lease terms—

Dear Sir or Madam:

We call your attention to paragraph (7) of the Lease Agreement between you as Landlord and the undersigned as Tenant, dated December 23, 1997, related to the premises located at 201 Wacker Drive, Suite 622. Pursuant to that paragraph, you are required to provide weekly office cleaning services.

As of the date of this letter, you have failed to perform as required in that no office cleaning services have been provided for the past four weeks. We hereby demand that you comply with such provision immediately.

BUYING, SELLING, AND RENTING MERCHANDISE AND EQUIPMENT

6

This chapter is written mostly for the benefit of the business that occasionally purchases, sells, or leases equipment, incidental to its regular business. The implications of selling and leasing equipment *as a business* are beyond the scope of this book. If you are in the business of selling or renting out equipment, you should do extra research to develop a comprehensive set of forms specific to your needs. As a practical matter, if you are purchasing from a dealer, the seller will usually have its own forms. Similarly, if you are renting equipment from someone in the business of renting equipment, the lessor with usually have its own forms.

However, you may find that you want to purchase, sell, rent from, or rent to, a friend, business acquaintance, family member, or business partner. For example, your tax advisor may suggest that, instead of having your business purchase a new computer, you would be better off buying a computer yourself and then leasing it to your company. (Perhaps this would allow your business more of a deduction for equipment rental payments than it would get from depreciating a computer the business owned). Whatever the reason, this chapter will help you with such occasional purchases, sales, and leases.

SALE OR PURCHASE OF EQUIPMENT ON AN INSTALLMENT PLAN

INSTALLMENT
SALE
DOCUMENTS

A simple cash purchase will usually just involve a bill of sale (see Sample Form 34). Several forms may be used in an installment sale. There may be a sales agreement (Sample Form 32), and often at least two other separate contracts are used to complete an installment sale: a security agreement (Sample Form 33), and a promissory note (see sample forms in chapter 8). If these are combined into one document, it keeps the note part from being negotiable. If the seller keeps a lien on the equipment as protection should the buyer fail to pay, then a Uniform Commercial Code financing statement (UCC-1) will be needed (see chapter 8). If the equipment is a motor vehicle or boat, there will be a different system for recording security liens. Prior to the sale, you may want to have the buyer complete a credit application, such as Form 23 in the appendix.

Sample Form 32. Sales agreement—

SALES AGREEMENT

This agreement is made by and between <u>Scrupulous Corporation</u>

<u> </u> (the "Seller") and

<u>   FBN, Inc. </u> , (the Buyer),

who agree as follows:

1. The Seller agrees to sell, and the Buyer agrees to buy:

    Scrupulous Model S-250 stamping machine,
    serial number S-97-20938547

2. In exchange for the Property, the Buyer agrees to pay to the Seller the sum of $<u> 30,000.00 </u>, payable according to the terms of a promissory note a copy of which is attached to this agreement and incorporated into this agreement by reference (the "Note").

3. The Seller retains a security interest in the Property to secure payment and performance of the Buyer's obligations under this agreement and the Note. Upon any default by the Buyer in the performance of any such obligations, the Seller may declare all obligations immediately due and payable and shall have the remedies of a secured party under the Uniform Commercial Code enacted in the state the laws of which govern the terms of this agreement.

This agreement is executed by the parties under seal on <u> June 6 </u>, <u>1998</u>.

Seller: Buyer:

Scrupulous Corporation   FBN, Inc.

Henry Hardy   *Marcia Bender*
Henry Hardy, President   Marcia Bender, President

Calvin Collier   *Matthew G. Bender*
Calvin Collier, Secretary   Matthew G. Bender, Secretary
(Corporate Seal)   (Corporate Seal)

Sample Form 33. Security agreement—

SECURITY AGREEMENT

In exchange for valuable consideration, the receipt and sufficiency of which is hereby acknowledged by the undersigned, _____FBN, Inc._____
(the "Debtor") hereby grants to _Scrupulous Corporation_____
(the "Creditor") a security interest in _Scrupulous Model S-250 stamping_____
_machine, serial number S-96-20938547_____.
to secure the payment and performance of the Debtor's obligations described as follows (the "Obligations"):

> To make payments pursuant to the Note between the parties, dated June 6, 1997.

Upon any default by the Debtor in the performance of any of the Obligations, the Creditor may declare all obligations of the Debtor immediately due and payable and shall have the remedies of a secured party under the Uniform Commercial Code enacted in the state the laws of which govern the terms of this agreement.

This agreement is executed by the parties under seal on _June 6, 1998._

Seller: Buyer:

Scrupulous Corporation   FBN, Inc.

By: *Henry Hardy*_____   By: *Marcia Bender*_____
Henry Hardy, President   Marcia Bender, President

Attest: *Calvin Collier*_____   Attest: *Matthew G. Bender*_____
Calvin Collier, Secretary   Matthew G. Bender, Secretary

(Corporate Seal)   (Corporate Seal)

The sales agreement will be accompanied by a promissory note. See chapter 8 for more information on promissory notes.

A bill of sale (Sample Form 34) is like a deed for property other than real estate. It is evidence that the buyer owns the property and that he or she bought it from the seller. It may also have some warranties from the seller, such as that the seller owned the property and had the right to sell it.

Sample Form 34. Bill of sale—

BILL OF SALE

For valuable consideration, the receipt and sufficiency of which is hereby acknowledged, the undersigned hereby sells and transfers to ___FBN, Inc.___

_____ the following:

```
1 Macintosh LC III computer, serial number 229458326, and
1 Macintosh LaserWriter Pro printer, serial number 492720-33927
```

The undersigned warrants and represents that it has good title to and full authority to sell and transfer the same and that the property is sold and transferred free and clear of all liens, claims and encumbrances except: None.

Executed under seal on ___June 6, 1998___.

Scrupulous Corporation

By: _*Henry Hardy*_____
       Henry Hardy, President

Attest:

_Calvin Collier_____
Calvin Collier, Secretary

(Corporate Seal)

Some buyers may insist on a warranty that specifically includes an indemnity provision. You will note that Form 22 in the appendix includes two bill of sale forms, one like that above and the other containing the following indemnity provision:

> "The undersigned warrants that, subject to the exceptions stated above, it will indemnify the Buyer, and defend title to the property, against the adverse claims of all persons."

VARIOUS CONTRACT WARRANTIES

Anyone who sells *goods* (which includes all kinds of merchandise and equipment) implies in so doing that the seller at least has title to the goods and the right to sell them.

Although the legal details that apply to implied and express warranties made by companies in the business of selling a particular item are beyond the scope of this book, a few words of warning may be helpful. If a seller is a merchant in the type of goods being sold, there are additional warranties implied under the Uniform Commercial Code, unless the seller disclaims them and sells the goods on an *as is* basis. If a merchant wants to go beyond implied warranties and make some specific promise about the nature or quality of the goods being sold, it is certainly possible to do so. But be careful. If you are in the business of selling consumer goods, you may be subject to the Magnuson-Moss Warranty Act passed by Congress in 1975. The act doesn't prevent you from making promises, but requires specific disclosures if you do. Anything less that a *full warranty* (which means, among other things, that you promise to provide free repairs or replacement of defective parts) must be labeled *limited warranty*. Needless to say, most express warranties are limited warranties. If you want to give a warranty with a product you are in the business of selling, check with your lawyer to make sure you are really promising what you intend to and that you have done it correctly.

Sample Form 35. Limited warranty—

LIMITED WARRANTY

The movement parts of your Scrupulous timepiece are warranted against defects in material and workmanship for five years to the initial consumer/owner from the date of purchase. All defective parts will be replaced with genuine factory parts at no charge for parts or labor. A handling charge of $8.00 will apply.

This Limited Warranty does not cover batteries, energy cells, case, crystal, strap or bracelet. This Limited Warranty does not cover damage resulting from accident, misuse, abuse, dirt, water or tampering.

This Limited Warranty gives you specific legal rights, and you may also have other rights which may vary from state to state. Except as otherwise required by law, this Limited Warranty is in lieu of all other warranties, conditions, guarantees or representations, express or implied. Scrupulous Corporation shall not be liable for incidental, consequential, special or indirect damages in connection with the product sold under this Limited Warranty or its use.

Sample Form 36. Warranty of title—

The seller warrants and represents that it has good title to and full authority to sell and transfer the property being sold and that the property is sold and transferred free and clear of all liens and encumbrances.

Sample Form 37. Disclaimer of warranty—

The seller disclaims any warranty of merchantability or fitness for a particular purpose. The property is sold in its present condition, "as is" and "where is."

CONSIGNMENT SALES

A consignment sale is one in which the owner gives something to another person for the purpose of selling it. The owner continues to own the item until it is actually sold, at which time the person in charge of selling it passes the purchase price on to the owner, usually subtracting a commission. Sample Form 38 is an agreement between the owner (the consignor) and the person in charge of selling the item (the consignee).

Occasionally, the consignee may go bankrupt, or have property taken to pay a judgment lien. To prevent this affecting the cosignor's property, consignors often require a financing statement (UCC-1) be filed so that there will be a public record of the consignor's ownership. (Also see the discussion of financing statements and Sample Form 47 in chapter 8.)

Sample Form 38. Consignment sale agreement—

CONSIGNMENT SALE AGREEMENT

This agreement is made by and between <u>Best Furniture, Inc.</u> (the "Consignor") and <u>Blanche Smith, d/b/a SalesMaster</u> (the "Consignee").

1. The Consignor and Consignee acknowledge and agree that the Consignor has provided the goods described below to Consignee for sale on a consignment basis, for the prices indicated, under the terms and conditions of this agreement:

    (14) Shelving units, Model #2433 $43.00 ea.
    (6) End tables, Model #2001 $48.00 ea.
    (2) Coffee tables, Model #2008 $61.00 ea.

2. The Consignee agrees to use its best efforts to sell the goods, for cash, for the benefit of the Consignor and to account to the Consignor for such sales within <u>90 days</u>, delivering the sale proceeds to the Consignor, less commission, at the time of the accounting.

3. The Consignee agrees to accept as its commission, in full payment for its performance under this agreement, an amount equal to <u>12</u>% of the gross sales price of the goods exclusive of any sales taxes.

4. If the Consignee shall be unable to sell any of such goods, they may be returned to the Consignor at the expense of the Consignee. The Consignor may reclaim unsold goods at any time.

5. At the request of the Consignor, the Consignee agrees to execute financing statements perfecting the Consignor's claim of ownership of the goods.

This agreement was executed by the parties on <u>December 18, 1998</u>.

Consignor: Best Furniture, Inc.   Consignee: Salesmaster

By: *Stella Martin*   By: *Blanche Smith*
    Stella Martin, President   Blanche Smith, Owner

EQUIPMENT RENTAL AGREEMENTS

Equipment leasing arrangements may really be an alternative method of financing the purchase of equipment. The lessee *leases* the equipment but expects to acquire ownership at the end of the lease term. The tax treatment of such arrangements is a complicated subject that can't be dealt with here. Sample Form 39 is for a relatively short term rental of equipment which will be returned to the lessor at the end of the term.

Sample Form 39. Equipment rental agreement—

PERSONAL PROPERTY LEASE AGREEMENT

This agreement is made by and between ___Scrupulous Corporation___ (the "Lessor") and ___Scrupulous Associates___ (the "Lessee").

1. The Lessor hereby leases to the Lessee, and the Lessee hereby leases from the lessor, beginning on __June 1, 1998__ and terminating on __Sept. 30, 1998__, the property described below (the "Property"):

CopyMate copier, Model #2500, Serial #6402748929328

2. In consideration of the leasing of the Property, the Lessee shall pay to the Lessor as rent the sum of $__100.00__ per month payable in advance on or before the __1st__ day of each month, the first such payment being due on __June 1, 1998__. Payment of rent shall be made to the Lessor at the following address:

201 Wacker Drive, Suite 622, Chicago, IL 60602

3. The Lessee agrees to use the Property in a careful manner and in compliance with applicable laws and regulations and, at the end of the lease term shall return the Property to the Lessor in the same condition as it was received by the Lessee, normal wear and tear excepted.

4. The Lessor shall not be liable to the Lessee for any liability, loss, or damage caused by the Property or its use that does not result directly and wholly from the negligence of the Lessor.

This agreement was executed by the parties on __May 25, 1998__.

Lessor: Scrupulous Corporation

Henry Hardy
_____
Henry Hardy, President

Calvin Collier
_____
Calvin Collier, Secretary
(Corporate Seal)

Lessee: Scrupulous Associates,
a general partnership

Roberta Moore
_____ (Seal)
Roberta Moore, Partner

_____

Uniform Commercial Code Transactions

The Uniform Commercial Code has been adopted by all states except Louisiana. The detailed requirement of the Code are beyond the scope of this book, however, there are a couple of forms you may find useful. The Code sets forth certain actions you may take in the event that goods you purchase do not conform to the specifications or requirements of what you ordered. Basically, you may either reject the goods, or accept them on certain conditions. Either way, you need to officially notify the seller. Form 32 in the appendix is a Notice of Rejection of Non-Conforming Goods, and Form 33 is a Notice of Conditional Acceptance of Non-Conforming Goods. In Form 32 you will need to describe or explain how the goods do not conform to what you ordered. In Form 33 you will need to explain how the goods do not conform, and you will also need to spell out the terms under which you will accept the non-conforming goods (such as for a reduction in the price, some corrective action on the part of the seller, etc.). If the seller does not agree with your terms, you will then need to send a notice of rejection.

SALE AND PURCHASE OF A BUSINESS 7

There are many different methods of acquiring a business other than starting from scratch and building it. Corporate mergers, stock purchases and asset purchases are the usual methods of acquiring an ongoing business. In a stock purchase, the acquirer will simply purchase most or all of the outstanding shares of a corporation. In the usual form, this means that the purchaser will negotiate the transaction with each existing shareholder of the target business. It works well if there is only one or a few shareholders, but presents obvious difficulties if there are many.

Most states now allow a *share exchange* procedure in which the shareholders of the target company vote on whether to sell their shares as a group. The procedure for a share exchange is very much like that for a merger. (See *The Most Valuable Corporate Forms You'll Ever Need*, by James C. Ray, published by Sourcebooks, Inc., for more on corporate mergers.) A stock purchase can also be accomplished through a tender offer, which is a more complicated process. You will need the services of an attorney if you are considering a share exchange or tender offer, so they will not be discussed in detail.

In an asset purchase, the acquirer buys most or all of the things owned by the target business and uses the assets to continue the business, leaving behind a shell more or less. The great thing about an asset purchase is that the buyer can pick and choose what it wants and leave behind the undesirable parts, including liabilities.

The tax implications of acquiring or disposing of a business are extremely complex and, these and other forms of acquisition should not be undertaken without ample expert advice.

A corporation involved in a stock or asset sale or purchase may require the approval of its shareholders. A share exchange will require the same sort of vote that a merger would. If a corporation sells all or substantially all its assets except "in the ordinary course of business," that too requires shareholder approval.

STOCK TRANSACTIONS

The usual stock transaction involves one corporation buying all the outstanding shares of another from one or several shareholders. The procedure is not different in concept from the procedure you would use to buy a house. After looking over the purchase and deciding it is what you want, you negotiate a deal. Frequently there is a *letter of intent*, or *agreement in principle*, which is a sort of preliminary agreement laying out the basic terms of the deal. It may be a legally binding contract even though it is short and informal, so treat it with respect. Sample Form 40, on the following page, is a typical example, drafted with the protection of the buyer in mind, which specifically claims that it is not legally binding as a contract. Even so, it may have legal consequences, so don't sign it unless you mean it.

Once there is a letter of intent, your lawyers will negotiate a more detailed agreement which will cover the items mentioned in the letter of intent and many others besides.

Sample Form 40. Letter of intent (stock transaction)—

Scrupulous Corporation

400 West 61st Avenue, P.O. Box 19, New York, NY 10032

October 18, 1998

Franklin Distributors, Inc.
4250 Hwy.
New York, NY 10036

Dear Mr. Franklin:

This letter will confirm the understanding reached between you as the proposed seller and the undersigned as the proposed buyer on October 16, 1998. This letter is not a legally binding contract for the sale and purchase of shares but only a description of the proposed arrangement by which the described transaction may take place.

Subject to the conditions stated in this letter, we have agreed in principle to buy and you have agreed to sell 100,000 common shares of Franklin Distributors, Inc. (the "Corporation"), being all of the outstanding shares of the Corporation (the "Shares") for a purchase price of $2.50 per share for a total of $250,000.00 payable in cash at the closing. Closing of the transaction and transfer of the shares will take place not later than December 1, 1998, at a time and place to be agreed upon by the parties.

Our interest in and any obligations with regard to such purchase is subject to the following conditions:

1. Between the date of this letter and up to the closing date, the Corporation will provide us and our advisors, employees and agents with an opportunity, at our expense, to perform a "due diligence" investigation and review of the Corporation's contracts, files, financial statements, accounts, stock record books, employee records and such other books and records as we may see fit. If, during the course of such investigations, we should uncover information reasonably leading us to conclude that the value of the Corporation, as of the date of closing, is materially less than the proposed purchase price, we may withdraw from the proposed purchase.

2. Our agreement to purchase the Shares shall be subject to the drafting and execution of a definitive sale and purchase agreement satisfactory to our legal counsel and approved in final form by our Board of Directors. Such agreement shall contain customary representations and warranties given by you regarding the accuracy of the Corporation's financial statements, the legal status of the corporation and its outstanding shares, material litigation, ownership of assets and other matters deemed of significance by us and our legal counsel in drafting such agreement.

3. Between the date of this letter and closing, the business of the Corporation will be conducted in the usual manner.

4. You and the Corporation will cooperate with us in any public announcements of the proposed sale and purchase deemed by our legal counsel to be required by law or otherwise desirable.

If this letter accurately states our understanding, please sign and date the enclosed copy and return it to us.

Very truly yours,

Scrupulous Corporation

By *Henry Hardy*
Henry Hardy, President

Accepted and agreed on: *10/20/98*
Distributors, Inc.

By *Milford Franklin*
Milford Franklin, President

ASSET TRANSACTIONS

In an asset transaction, instead of buying shares of stock, you are buying a list of individual items—desks, computers, paper clips, trucks, etc. It may be that some of these assets are transferable only by way of special documentation. For example, if you are buying the target's fleet of automobiles, you have to deal with the title documents peculiar to motor vehicles. If you are buying the target's real estate, deeds must be recorded, and if you are buying shares of stock that the target owns, the share certificates must be endorsed and the transfer recorded by the issuing corporation. So an asset transaction may involve a formidable stack of documents.

Nevertheless, the same basic documents involved in a typical stock transaction will be somewhere in the stack. Sample form 41, on the following page, is the body of a letter of intent for an asset transaction.

Sample Form 41. Letter of intent (asset transaction)—

Dear Mr. Franklin:

This letter will confirm the understanding reached between you as the proposed seller and the undersigned as the proposed buyer on October 16, 1998. This letter is not a legally binding contract for the sale and purchase of assets but only a description of the proposed arrangement by which the described transaction may take place.

Subject to the conditions stated in this letter, we have agreed in principle to buy and you have agreed to sell all of the assets (the "Assets") of Franklin Distributors, Inc. (the "Corporation") for a purchase price of $250,000.00, payable in cash at the closing. Closing of the transaction and transfer of the assets will take place not later than December 1, 1998, at a time and place to be agreed upon by the parties.

Such sale and purchase is subject to the following conditions:

1. Between the date of this letter and the closing date, the Corporation will provide us and our advisors, employees and agents with an opportunity at our expense to perform a "due diligence" investigation and review of any and all of the Corporation's books and records as we may see fit. If, such investigation uncovers information reasonably leading us to conclude that the value of the Assets, as of the date of closing, is materially less than the proposed purchase price, we may withdraw from the proposed purchase.

2. Our agreement to purchase the Assets shall be subject to the drafting and execution of a definitive sale and purchase agreement satisfactory to our legal counsel and approved in final form by our Board of Directors. Such agreement shall contain a definitive list of the assets purchased and customary representations and warranties given by you regarding the value of the Assets and their ownership and other matters deemed of significance by us and our legal counsel in drafting such agreement.

3. Between the date of this letter and closing, the business of the Corporation will be conducted in the usual manner.

4. You and the Corporation will cooperate with us in any public announcements of the proposed sale and purchase deemed by our legal counsel to be required by law or otherwise desirable.

If this letter accurately states our understanding, please sign and date the enclosed copy and return it to us.

Very truly yours,

Scrupulous Corporation

By _Henry Hardy_____
Henry Hardy, President

Accepted and agreed on:_*10/20/98*_____
Franklin Distributors, Inc.

By _Milford Franklin_____
Milford Franklin, President

BULK SALES   One of the advantages of an asset transaction mentioned above is that the buyer can leave undesirable assets and liabilities of the seller behind and purchase only the assets the buyer really wants. This is in contrast to a merger or stock acquisition in which the buyer acquires the target warts and all, becoming responsible for the target's liabilities at the same time it acquires the target's assets. There is a danger then, that in an asset deal, a corporation might keep its debts while giving up all the assets it could use to pay the debts, thus cheating its creditors. The states have enacted *bulk sales* statutes as a safeguard for creditors in such situations. The statutes require that a company selling most of its assets must give fair notice to its creditors so they can take steps to protect themselves. If the requirements of the statute are not followed precisely, the buyer will find itself responsible for the seller's debts whether it wants them or not. This is one big reason to consult a lawyer before completing such a transaction.

DISSENTING   As with mergers and share exchanges, shareholders of a corporation
SHAREHOLDERS   selling substantially all of its assets will have dissenters' rights. (See chapter 10 of *The Most Valuable Corporate Forms You'll Ever Need*, by James C. Ray, published by Sourcebooks, Inc.)

BORROWING AND LENDING MONEY 8

PROMISSORY NOTES

NEGOTIABILITY

A note is *negotiable* if the promise to pay the money is not subject to any conditions, if it is written and signed, if it is payable to a named person or a person to whom the note has been *negotiated* (sold) or to the *bearer* or *holder* of the note, and if it is to be paid either on a specified date or on the demand of the person the debt is to be paid to. These requirements account for some of the odd language that notes and other negotiable instruments, such as checks, use. For example, the words "pay to the order of" mean that the person who owes the money has to pay it to the person named or to whomever that person orders it to be paid—that is, to whomever it has been negotiated. There are other kinds of contracts that create an obligation to repay money, but promissory notes are the most reliable and readily enforceable.

METHOD OF PAYMENT

Promissory notes can be simple or quite complex with many different arrangements for interest rates and repayment. Sample Form 42 is an example of a completed promissory note for repayment on demand of the holder of the note. This uses Form 24 from the appendix, with the appropriate language typed in for this type of repayment. Sample Forms 43, 44 and 45 are examples of the language to be filled in on Form 24 in the appendix for various other methods of repayment.

A word of caution: Do not sign duplicate copies of a promissory note! Each signed note is an enforceable promise to pay the money referred to in the note. So if you sign three copies of the same note, you have promised to pay the same amount of money three times. Even machine copies of a note should be made before the note is signed (and the copy should not be signed, of course) so there won't be any mistakes.

Sample Form 42. Promissory note (payment on demand)—

NOTE

$ __10,000.00__   Date: July 1, 1998

__Scrupulous Corporation__ hereby promises to pay to the order of __Roberta Moore__ the sum of $__10,000.00__ with interest thereon from the date of this note to the date of payment at the rate of interest per annum as set forth below:

This note shall bear interest at the rate of 12% per annum on any unpaid balance. This note is payable upon demand of the holder made in writing to the undersigned at the address listed below.

This note is due a payable in full on __demand of the holder__, if not paid sooner. The principal and interest shall be payable when due at __400 West 61st Avenue, P.O. Box 19, New York, NY 10032__ or at a place of which the undersigned may be notified in writing by the holder of this note.

This note is not assumable without the written consent of the lender. This note may be paid in whole or in part at any time prior without penalty. The borrower waives demand, presentment, protest, and notice. This note shall be fully payable upon demand of any holder in the event the undersigned shall default on the terms of this note or any agreement securing the payment of this note. In the event of default, the undersigned agrees to pay all costs of collection including reasonable attorneys fees.

❑ This note is given in payment for the purchase of personal property and is secured by a security interest in such property.

Scrupulous Corporation

By: __*Henry Hardy*__
Henry Hardy, President

Attest: __*Calvin Collier*__
Calvin Collier, Secretary
(Corporate Seal)

Sample Form 43. Promissory note (due on specific date)—

> This note shall bear interest at the rate of 12% per annum on any unpaid balance.
>
> This note is due a payable in full on ___July 1, 2006_____, if not paid sooner.

Sample Form 44. Promissory note (installment payments)—

> This note shall bear interest at the rate of 12% per annum on any unpaid balance. The principal and interest shall be payable in equal monthly installments of $222.45 each, beginning on August 1, 1998, and continuing on the 1st day of each month thereafter.

Sample Form 45. Promissory Note (balloon payment)—

> This note shall bear interest at the rate of 12% per annum. The principal and interest shall be payable in equal monthly installments of $143.48 each, beginning on August 1, 1998 and continuing on the 1st day of each month thereafter until August 1, 2001 at which time the entire balance shall become due and payable.

INTEREST CALCULATIONS

There must be an infinite number of ways to calculate interest on a loan. The previous four examples provide for a basic fixed rate. Sample Form 46 provides for the rate to increase each year. This might be used as an incentive for early repayment. Another method is to peg the rate to the prime rate of a designated bank.

Sample Form 46. Promissory note (increasing interest rate)—

> From the date of this note to the first anniversary of such date at the rate of 8%.
>
> From the first anniversary of this note to the second anniversary at the rate of 10%.
>
> From the second anniversary of this note to the third anniversary at the rate of 12%.

SECURING THE LOAN

If payment of a loan is to be secured by a lien on some piece of property, an agreement separate from the promissory note is needed. Sample Form 33 in chapter 6 is an example of a security agreement creating a security interest in a piece of personal property. Regarding security interests in real property, see chapter 5.

A security agreement establishes a relationship between the borrower and lender, that is, the borrower has designated some property as security and given the lender power to sell the property in satisfaction of the debt in case the borrower defaults. But what is to keep the borrower from selling the collateral to a third party before the loan is in default or before the lender has a chance to foreclose on the collateral? It would be unfair for an innocent third party purchaser of the collateral to lose the property he or she has paid good money for just because the borrower has breached his contract with the lender. In fact the Uniform Commercial Code usually protects the innocent *good faith purchaser* in such circumstances, and the lender loses his or her rights to the collateral.

How can the lender be protected? By making sure that third parties will know—or at least have an opportunity to learn—that there is a security agreement in effect. This is called *perfecting* a security interest. One way to perfect a security interest is for the lender to take physical possession of the collateral as in a pawn shop transaction. Another way is for the lender to file a public notice of the security agreement on form UCC-1. A UCC-1 or *financing statement* (Sample Form 47) is filed with some designated official that the property described in the notice serves as collateral for a loan. Each state has its own UCC-1 form (California's form is used in the example below). Where the statement should be filed depends on the type of collateral and on state law. Your state will have a preferred or required form, a centralized filing system (usually in the office of the Secretary of State), and a local filing system. If you are the seller, be sure you file in the right place. You may have to file in both places. If the collateral is a motor vehicle or boat, there will be a different system for recording security liens.

Sample Form 47. UCC-1 Financing Statement—

COMMERCIAL CODE FORMS
See also topics Chattel Mortgages and Commercial Code.

Financing Statement.—
This **FINANCING STATEMENT** is presented for filing and will remain effective with certain exceptions for a period of five years from the date of filing pursuant to section 9403 of the California Uniform Commercial Code.

1. DEBTOR (LAST NAME FIRST—IF AN INDIVIDUAL)	1A. SOCIAL SECURITY OR FEDERAL TAX NO.
FBN, Inc.	59-682215

1B. MAILING ADDRESS	1C. CITY, STATE	1D. ZIP CODE
P.O. Box 27198	Fresno, CA	93706

2. ADDITIONAL DEBTOR (IF ANY) (LAST NAME FIRST—IF AN INDIVIDUAL)	2A. SOCIAL SECURITY OR FEDERAL TAX NO.

2B. MAILING ADDRESS	2C. CITY, STATE	2D. ZIP CODE

3. DEBTOR'S TRADE NAMES OR STYLES (IF ANY)	3A. FEDERAL TAX NUMBER

4. SECURED PARTY	4A. SOCIAL SECURITY NO., FEDERAL TAX NO. OR BANK TRANSIT AND A.B.A. NO.
NAME Scrupulous Corporation MAILING ADDRESS 400 West 61st Ave. CITY New York STATE NY 10032 ZIP CODE	59-016599

5. ASSIGNEE OF SECURED PARTY (IF ANY)	5A. SOCIAL SECURITY NO., FEDERAL TAX NO. OR BANK TRANSIT AND A.B.A. NO.
NAME MAILING ADDRESS CITY STATE ZIP CODE	

6. This FINANCING STATEMENT covers the following types or items of property (include description of real property on which located and owner of record when **required by Instruction 4**).

Scrupulous Model S-250 stamping machine, Serial #S-96-20938547

7. CHECK ☒ IF APPLICABLE	7A. ☐ PRODUCTS OF COLLATERAL ARE ALSO COVERED	7B. DEBTOR(S) SIGNATURE NOT REQUIRED IN ACCORDANCE WITH INSTRUCTION 5(a) ITEM: ☒ (1) ☐ (2) ☐ (3) ☐ (4)

8. CHECK ☒ IF APPLICABLE	☐ DEBTOR IS A "TRANSMITTING UTILITY" IN ACCORDANCE WITH UCC § 9105 (1) (n)

9. ▸ *Marcia Bender, President* DATE: 6/6/98	CODE	10. THIS SPACE FOR USE OF FILING OFFICER (DATE, TIME, FILE NUMBER AND FILING OFFICER)
SIGNATURE(S) OF DEBTOR(S)		
Marcia Bender, President, FBN, Inc. TYPE OR PRINT NAME(S) OF DEBTOR(S)	1	
	2	
▸ *Henry Hardy, President* SIGNATURE(S) OF SECURED PARTY(IES)	3	
	4	
Henry Hardy, President, Scrupulous Corporation TYPE OR PRINT NAME(S) OF SECURED PARTY(IES)	5	
11. *Return copy to:*	6	
NAME ⌐ Scrupulous Corporation ⌐ ADDRESS CITY 400 West 61st Ave. STATE ZIP CODE ⌊ New York, NY 10032 ⌋	7 8 9 0	

FORM UCC-1—
Approved by the Secretary of State

DEBT
ASSIGNMENTS

As explained at the beginning of this chapter, one of the important attributes of a promissory note is its negotiability. When a note is *negotiated* (sold or otherwise transferred), it is important for the new owner to notify the borrower that future payments should be made to him or her. See chapter 1 for more information about the assignment of contracts and the need for appropriate notice. Sample Form 48 is such a notice to a debtor.

Sample Form 48. Notice of assignment of debt—

Notice of Assignment of Debt

To: FBN, Inc.

     You are hereby notified that Scrupulous Corporation has assigned and sold to National Service, Inc., its rights pursuant to your promissory note dated June 6, 1998, and that your debt in the amount of $30,000.00 is now owed to the undersigned. All future payments should be directed to the undersigned to insure credit for payment.

Peter J. Piper
_____
Peter J. Piper, President
National Service, Inc.
1423 W. 73rd Street
New York, NY 10034

COMPLETION OF
PAYMENTS

Discharge of Promissory Note. Once a loan is completely paid, it is good practice for the original note to be returned to the borrower with a notation by the lender that it has been paid. Rather than destroy the original, the borrower should keep the original note with the lender's notation. That way you have written evidence that the lender has accepted final payment. Sample Form 49, if written on the face of the note by an authorized agent of the lender, will cancel the note.

Sample Form 49. Cancellation of note—

THIS NOTE WAS PAID AND SATISFIED IN FULL BY THE BORROWER ON MAY 23, 2000.

National Service, Inc.
By: *Peter J. Piper*
_____
Peter J. Piper, President

Basic Discharge of Security Interest. When a note is paid and the loan discharged, any related security interest is automatically discharged as well. There are some occasions on which a lender and borrower will agree to cancel a security arrangement even though the underlying debt has not been paid. For example, a new form of security may be substituted for the existing arrangement.

Sample Form 50 provides written evidence that the security interest has been discharged.

Sample Form 50. Release of security interest—

```
              Discharge of Security Interest

    FOR VALUE RECEIVED, the undersigned hereby releases and dis-
charges a security interest granted by FBN, Inc., to the under-
signed pursuant to a security agreement dated September 16, 1998.
This discharge shall constitute a discharge of the obligation for
which such security interest was granted.

    This discharge was executed on November 22, 1989.

                                  Scrupulous Corporation


                                  By  Henry Hardy
                                  _____
                                  Henry Hardy, President
```

Discharge of UCC Financing Statement. If a UCC financing statement was filed, you will also need to file a UCC termination statement. Again, each state has its own form, which may be designated "UCC-2," "UCC-3," or be part of the UCC-1 itself. This will have the effect of clearing the form UCC-1 financing statement from the record. Sample Form 51, on the following page, is an example of the form used in California.

Sample Form 51. UCC Termination of security interest—

Statement of Continuation, Termination, Etc.—
This STATEMENT is presented for filing pursuant to the California Uniform Commercial Code

1. FILE NO. OF ORIG. FINANCING STATEMENT 96-25179	1A. DATE OF FILING OF ORIG. FINANCING STATEMENT 6/7/98	1B. DATE OF ORIG. FINANCING STATEMENT 6/6/98	1C. PLACE OF FILING ORIG. FINANCING STATEMENT Fresno

2. DEBTOR (LAST NAME FIRST) FBN, Inc.	2A. SOCIAL SECURITY NO., FEDERAL TAX NO. 59-682215	

2B. MAILING ADDRESS P.O. Box 27198	2C. CITY, STATE Fresno, CA	2D. ZIP CODE 93706

3. ADDITIONAL DEBTOR (IF ANY) (LAST NAME FIRST)	3A. SOCIAL SECURITY OR FEDERAL TAX NO.	

3B. MAILING ADDRESS	3C. CITY, STATE	3D. ZIP CODE

4. SECURED PARTY NAME Scrupulous Corporation MAILING ADDRESS 400 West 61st Ave. CITY New York STATE NY 10032 ZIP CODE	4A. SOCIAL SECURITY NO., FEDERAL TAX NO. OR BANK TRANSIT AND A.B.A. NO. 59-016599

5. ASSIGNEE OF SECURED PARTY (IF ANY) NAME MAILING ADDRESS CITY STATE ZIP CODE	5A. SOCIAL SECURITY NO., FEDERAL TAX NO. OR BANK TRANSIT AND A.B.A. NO.

6.

A ☐ CONTINUATION—The original Financing Statement between the foregoing Debtor and Secured Party bearing the file number and date shown above is continued. If collateral is crops or timber, check here ☐ and insert description of real property on which growing or to be grown in Item 7 below.

B ☐ RELEASE—From the collateral described in the Financing Statement bearing the file number shown above, the Secured Party releases the collateral described in Item 7 below.

C ☐ ASSIGNMENT—The Secured Party certifies that the Secured Party has assigned to the Assignee above named, all the Secured Party's rights under the Financing Statement bearing the file number shown above in the collateral described in Item 7 below.

D ☒ TERMINATION—The Secured Party certifies that the Secured Party no longer claims a security interest under the Financing Statement bearing the file number shown above.

E ☐ AMENDMENT—The Financing Statement bearing the file number shown above is amended as set forth in Item 7 below. (Signature of Debtor required on all amendments.)

F ☐ OTHER

7.

8. (Date) Oct. 23 19 2000	CODE	9. This Space for Use of Filing Officer (Date, Time, Filing Office)
By: *Marcia Bender* President SIGNATURE(S) OF DEBTOR(S) (TITLE)	1 2	
By: *Henry Hardy* President SIGNATURE(S) OF SECURED PARTY(IES) (TITLE)	3 4	

10. Return Copy to	5
NAME ADDRESS CITY AND STATE ⌈ FBN, Inc. P.O. Box 27198 Fresno, CA 93706 ⌉	6 7 8 9

(1) Filing Officer Copy
STANDARD FORM — FILING FEE $5.00   UNIFORM COMMERCIAL CODE — FORM UCC-2
Approved by the Secretary of State

DELINQUENT ACCOUNTS

If the buyer does not pay, there are various actions you may pursue. These range from a letter demanding payment to hiring a collection agency to filing a lawsuit. Some businesses send more than one demand letter before resorting to a lawsuit. One view is that lawsuits are expensive and time-consuming, and it is better to make numerous attempts to get payment voluntarily first. The other view is that multiple demand letters send a message to the debtor that you are not serious about collection, and are merely making empty threats. If word gets around that you send one letter, then sue, your debtors may take you more seriously.

Sample Form 52 is a demand letter, which states that the next step is a lawsuit. If you want to send more than one, you can simply modify it to delete or replace the language threatening a lawsuit, and indicate that it is a "Second Notice," "Third Notice," etc. The form as it is can then be designated the "Final Notice."

Sample Form 52.   Demand letter—

DEMAND FOR PAYMENT

Date: February 3, 1998

TO: NSF Corporation
           52 S. First Street
           St. Louis, MO

Your account is delinquent in the amount of $ February 3, 1998.

Please be advised that in the event we do not receive payment in full within 14 days of the date of this notice, we will initiate collection proceedings against you without further notice. If such proceedings are initiated, you will also be responsible for pre-judgment interest, attorneys' fees, court costs, and any and all other costs of collection. Collection proceedings may also adversely affect your credit rating.

If full payment has already been sent, please disregard this notice.

Please contact the undersigned if you have any questions.

Henry Hardy

Henry Hardy, President
Scrupulous Corporation

If you decide to hire a collection agency, you can use Form 35 in the appendix to notify the debtor. Sample Form 53 is a completed example of this form.

Sample Form 53.   Notice of Assignment of Account for Collection—

NOTICE OF ASSIGNMENT OF ACCOUNT FOR COLLECTION

Date: <u>February 19, 1998</u>

TO: NSF Corporation
           52 S. First Street
           St. Louis, MO

Please be advised that your delinquent account has been assigned for collection to the following collection agent: <u>Debt Collection Associates, Inc.,</u>
<u>415 Strongarme Street, St. Louis, MO</u>   .
The amount assigned is based upon the following amount(s):

        $,795.45, representing the amount owed for goods
        delivered pursuant to contract dated October 1,
        1996, plus accrued interest.

Please contact the above-mentioned collection agent regarding this notice and all future payments on this account.

                              Henry Hardy
                              _____
                              Henry Hardy, President
                              Scrupulous Corporation

FILING A   If you wish to file suit yourself, you should either hire a lawyer or look
LAWSUIT   for a self-help law book appropriate for your state and the amount of
              your claim. Each state's court system usually has divisions based upon
              the type and the amount of the claim. For example, there may be a
              small claims court, a landlord/tenant court, etc.

AVOIDING LIABILITY AND SETTLING DISPUTES 9

PROTECTING AGAINST LIABILITY BEFORE IT ARISES

DISCLAIMERS OF
LIABILITY

It's not unusual that a business will undertake something which everyone recognizes could go wrong, causing an injury. When all parties go into a contract with eyes open, fully informed, and understanding the risks, it is only fair that the person who bears potential liability have the ability to bargain away that risk. Form 54 is an acknowledgment by the customer who may be injured in a risky undertaking that he or she is aware of the risks and undertakes them willingly, releasing the business of liability for any resulting injury.

How far can you go? As a rule of thumb, the person who agrees to a disclaimer such as the one below, assumes only the risks that are specified in the release or the ones that are reasonably foreseeable. For example, suppose the company is in the business of renting parachutes to skydivers. A skydiver may reasonably foresee that, no matter how good the equipment is, a jump may go wrong. Knowing this, he or she may be expected to release the equipment renter from liability for injuries resulting from the jump. But does that include a release from liability if the equipment company negligently employs a parachute packer who gets drunk and does a poor job of preparing the equipment or fails to notice a fatal rip in the parachute's fabric? Probably not. But what if the release specifically states that the renter will not be responsible for torn or poorly packed parachutes prepared by drunken workers? Would the release be valid? Maybe, but who would knowingly sign such a thing?

A disclaimer such as this should be viewed as a sort of warning sign saying, "Here are the things that could go wrong. We are warning you about them in advance and letting you know we can't be responsible for such things, because we can't control them. You are responsible for your own injuries if you do this thing." A disclaimer will have a chance of being effective only if the person who agrees to it has a fair chance to read and understand it. A disclaimer won't help you if you try to disguise it or hide it.

Sample Form 54, on the following page, is a waiver and assumption of risk which an individual customer will sign agreeing to assume the full risk for the use of certain facilities and for engaging in certain activities. The customer acknowledges that he or she is aware of the dangers inherent in the activity, and agrees to release the business from liability for injuries or damages that may result.

Sample Form 54.   Waiver and Assumption of Risk—

WAIVER AND ASSUMPTION OF RISK

I, _____, hereby voluntarily sign this Waiver and Assumption of Risk in favor of __Deep-C Divers, Inc._____ (the "Company"), fully waiving and releasing the Company from any and all claims for personal injury, property damage, or death that may result from my use of the Company's facilities or property, or from my participation in the following activities or instruction ("activities"):

```
SCUBA diving and snorkeling, including but not limited
to instruction from the company's employees, and use of
the Company's swimming pool, boat, dock, and diving and
snorkeling equipment.
```

I sign this Waiver and Assumption of Risk in consideration of the opportunity to use the Company's facilities or property, receive instruction from the Company and its employees, or to participate in Company-sponsored activities as described above.

I acknowledge and understand that there are dangers and risks associated with the activities described above, which have been fully explained to me. I fully assume the dangers and risks, and agree to use my best judgment in engaging in those activities and to follow the safety instructions provided.

I am a competent adult, aged _____, and I freely and voluntarily assume the risks associated with the activities described above.

Dated:_____

Witness:_____   _____

                                                Name:_____
                                                Address:_____

                                                _____
                                                Telephone:_____

In case of emergency, please contact:
Name:_____   Address:_____
Relationship:_____
Telephone:_____   _____

Sample Form 55 is a contract under which a corporation agrees to provide services as an independent contractor to a customer. It warns the customer of dangers inherent in the service to be performed, and the customer agrees to release the business from liability for injuries or damages that may result from the performance of the services.

Sample Form 55. Contract for services (with disclaimer and release from liability)—

CONTRACT FOR SERVICES

This agreement is made between_____Scrupulous Corporation_____ (the "Company") and ___Developers, Inc.____, (the "Customer"). The Company and the Customer agree as follows:

1. The Company will provide the following services to the Customer under the terms and conditions of this agreement:

Removal and disposal of one underground storage tank.

2. The Company agrees to perform such services diligently using its best efforts and providing competent personnel and adequate time to complete the work to professional standards of high quality. The Company may perform such services at the times and locations as may be agreed by the parties.

3. As payment for the completed services described above, and in addition to the release provided in paragraph 5 below, the Customer shall pay to the Company the sum of $__1,750.00____payable in the following manner:

50% upon commencement of work, and the balance upon completion.

4. The services to be provided by the Company shall begin not later than_May 1, 1998,_and shall be completed not later than_May 15, 1998._

5. DISCLAIMER OF LIABILITY AND RELEASE BY CUSTOMER—READ CAREFULLY: The Company has informed the Customer, and the Customer acknowledges having been informed that the performance of the services described above involves certain inherent risks and dangers including, but not limited to the following: Leakage or spillage of material remaining in tank, and subsidence of adjacent ground and roadway.

THE COMPANY DISCLAIMS ALL LIABILITY FOR DAMAGES AND INJURIES THAT MAY RESULT FROM ALL RISKS REFERRED TO IN THIS PARAGRAPH, and the Customer, having been so informed, in further consideration of the Company's willingness to provide such services, hereby releases, discharges and acquits the Company, and its employees, agents, successors and assigns, from any and all claims, actions, suits, or liabilities that may arise as a result of or in connection with the performance of the services not resulting directly and wholly from the negligence of the Company, its agents and employees.

6. The parties agree that no employer - employee relationship is created by this agreement, but that the relationship of the Company to the Customer shall be that of an independent contractor.

This agreement was executed by the parties on ____April 25, 1996____.

Scrupulous Corporation   Developers, Inc.

By: _*Henry Hardy*_____   By: _*Ronald Bumpp*_____

Henry Hardy, President   Ronald Bumpp, President

INDEMNIFICATION While the disclaimer and release assures the Company it will not be liable for certain damages, it does nothing to protect the Company from liabilities that may nevertheless arise, either because the disclaimer is not broad enough or because the liabilities are such that they cannot be reasonably disclaimed. That is the purpose of an indemnification agreement such as Sample Form 56. Remember that an indemnification is of no value if the indemnifier ("indemnitor") has no funds to pay it with, so be careful who signs the agreement. You may want it signed by a corporation and also the shareholders, if you can get it. (*The Most Valuable Corporate Forms You'll Ever Need* covers indemnification of corporate officers and directors.)

Sample Form 56. Agreement for indemnification—

INDEMNIFICATION AGREEMENT

In exchange for _the Company allowing use of its property by the undersigned as described below_ and other valuable consideration, the receipt and sufficiency of which is hereby acknowledged, the undersigned hereby agrees to indemnify and hold Scrupulous Corporation (the "Company") harmless from any claim, action, liability or suit arising out of or in any way connected with the following: the operation by Unified Charities, Inc., and CarniProductions, Inc., of a charity-benefit carnival, including but not limited to the operation of amusement rides, food concessions, and fireworks displays, on the Company's property on February 14 and 15, 1999, including set-up on February 13, 1999 and tear-down on February 16, 1999.

In the event any claim reasonably believed by the Company to be subject to indemnification under this agreement is asserted against the Company, the Company will provide timely notice of such claim to the undersigned. The undersigned will thereafter, at its own expense, defend and protect the Company against such claim. Should the undersigned be unable or fail to so defend the Company, the Company shall have the right to defend or settle such claim, and the undersigned shall reimburse the Company for all settlements, judgments, fees, costs, expenses and payments, including reasonable attorneys' fees, incurred by the Company in connection with the discharge of such claim.

This agreement is binding upon and shall inure to the benefit of the parties, their successors, assigns and personal representatives.

Executed under seal on _January 12, 1998_ .

Unified Charities, Inc.   CarniProductions, Inc.

James Gooddeed   *Barnum N. Bayley*
James Gooddeed, President   Barnum N. Bayley, President

Marcy Hopewell   *Buffy Ringling*
Marcy Hopewell, Secretary   Buffy Ringling, Secretary
(Corporate Seal)   (Corporate Seal)

DISCHARGING LIABILITY AFTER IT ARISES

A liability is a debt owed. Like other debts, liabilities of tort (personal injury) or contract can be discharged in various ways, including the payment of money or promise to pay money. Sample Form 57 is a release from all liabilities that the person released may owe to the signer, while Sample Form 58 is limited to matters related to a specific event or contract. In Sample Form 59 the parties release each other from liabilities.

Sample Form 57. General release of liability—

GENERAL RELEASE

In exchange for the sum of $10.00 and other valuable consideration, the receipt and sufficiency of which is hereby acknowledged, the undersigned hereby forever releases, discharges and acquits <u>Nationwide Carrier Corporation</u>, and [its/~~his/her~~] successors, assigns, heirs and personal representatives, from any and all claims, actions, suits, agreements or liabilities in favor of or owed to the undersigned, existing at any time up to the date of this release.

IN WITNESS WHEREOF, the undersigned has executed this release under seal on<u> May 8, 1998.</u>

Scrupulous Corporation

By: <u>*Henry Hardy*</u>

Henry Hardy, President

Attest:
<u>*Calvin Collier*</u>

Calvin Collier, Secretary

(Corporate Seal)

Sample Form 58. Specific release of liability—

SPECIFIC RELEASE

In exchange for the sum of $10.00 and other valuable consideration, the receipt and sufficiency of which is hereby acknowledged, the undersigned hereby forever releases, discharges and acquits <u>Scrupulous Corporation</u>, and [its/~~his/her~~] successors, assigns, heirs and personal representatives, from any and all claims, actions, suits, agreements or liabilities arising out of or related to:
any and all injuries and damages sustained by the undersigned, pursuant to the undersigned slipping and falling at the premises of Scrupulous Corporation on July 4, 1998.

IN WITNESS WHEREOF, the undersigned has executed this release under seal on<u> August 28, 1998.</u>

<u>*Justin Cayce*</u>

Justin Cayce

Sample Form 59. Mutual release of liability—

MUTUAL RELEASE

In exchange for the sum of $10.00 and other valuable consideration, the receipt and sufficiency of which is hereby acknowledged, the undersigned hereby forever release, discharge and acquit each other, and their successors, assigns, heirs and personal representatives, from any and all claims, actions, suits, agreements or liabilities arising out of or related to: the contract executed by and between the parties on March 3, 1998.

IN WITNESS WHEREOF, the undersigned have executed this release under seal and by authority of their respective boards of directors as of October 27, 1998.

Western Distributors, Inc.

Jackson Miller
_____
Jackson Miller, President

David Jones
_____
David Jones, Secretary
(Corporate Seal)

Mountain Packaging,
a general partnership
Marilyn Kim
_____
Marilyn Kim, general partner

MECHANICS' AND MATERIALMEN'S LIENS

Your state will have a statute that protects various workers from customers who don't pay. If you take your car in for repairs and then refuse to pay for the work done, the mechanic will have an automatic statutory lien on the vehicle for the amount of the repairs. If you persist in not paying, this means the mechanic can sell your car and apply the proceeds to the outstanding bill. The same is true of building contractors and suppliers.

It frequently becomes important for such automatic liens to be released (and proven in writing to be released) so that, for example, a new house can be sold free of any such liens. Sample Form 60 is an example of such a form. Presented to the purchaser it will show that the building is free of any such liens from the contractor of supplier who signs it. If a lien has already be recorded, it will be necessary to use a form that refers to the book and page (or other appropriate recording information used in your state) where the lien was recorded.

Sample Form 60. Release of mechanic's and materialmen's liens—

RELEASE OF LIENS

The undersigned [sub]contractor has furnished construction materials and/or labor in connection with repairs or construction at the site known as 9834 W. Washington Ave., St. Paul, MN (the "Premises"). The undersigned hereby releases all liens and rights to file liens against the Premises for any and all such materials or services provided through the date of this release.

The date of this release is January 2, 1998 .

Contractor/Subcontractor:
Carl Nales, d/b/a Carl the Carpenter

Carl Nales
Carl Nales

AGREEMENTS NOT TO BRING LAWSUITS

There is a difference between (a) agreeing that one person has no further claim of liability against another and (b) promising that, although there may be a claim, the person will not bring a law suit based on it. The former is a release, and the latter is a covenant not to sue. Once a claim has been released it no longer exists and (unless there has been fraud involved) can't be revived. But if you promise not to sue on a claim, the claim doesn't go away, you've just promised not to try to enforce it. If the promise not to sue goes away, the claim is still there, ready to be enforced.

If a claimant receives cash in an agreed settlement of the claim, it is appropriate to give a release. There will never be any need to enforce a debt that has been fully paid. If you only have a promise to pay something in the future, such as a promissory note, then maybe a "covenant not to sue" is appropriate. The claimant promises not to bring a law suit on the claim as long as the note is not in default.

Sample Form 61. Covenant not to sue—

COVENANT NOT TO SUE

This agreement is made by and between ___Justin Cayce___
(the "Covenantor"), for [itself/himself/herself] and for its heirs, legal representatives and assigns, and ___Scrupulous Corporation___ (the "Covenantee").

1. In exchange for the Covenantor's covenant herein, the Covenantee ___promises and agrees to pay all of the Coventor's medical bills and $50 per day for lost wages arising out of injuries Covenantor received on July 4, 1998 at the Covenantee's premises.___

2. In exchange for the consideration stated in paragraph 1 above, the receipt and sufficiency of which is hereby acknowledged by the Covenantor, the Covenantor covenants with the Covenantee never to institute any suit or action at law or in equity against the Covenantee by reason of any claim the Covenantor now has or may hereafter acquire related to: ___injuries Covenantor received on July 4, 1998 at the Covenantee's premises___.

This agreement was executed by the parties under seal on ___August 15, 1998___.

Covenantor: Covenantee:

                                               Scrupulous Corporation

Justin Cayce   _Henry Hardy_
Justin Cayce   Henry Hardy, President

                                               Calvin Collier
                                               Calvin Collier, Secretary

                                               (Corporate Seal)

JUDGMENTS   If you already have a court judgment against you, it will eventually become necessary to get released from the judgment, either because you have paid it or because you have reached some kind of agreement with the person or company with the judgment against you. Sample Form 62 is an example of a release of judgment. Form 44 in the appendix is a blank release form. You will need to complete the top portion of the form so that it matches what is on the judgment itself. This will typically include an identification of the court, the names of the parties, and a case number. You should also check to be sure the form you prepare complies with the requirements of your state and county for recording.

Sample Form 62. Release of judgment—

IN THE CIRCUIT COURT OF THE STATE OF OREGON
THE COUNTY OF CLACKAMAS

Oregon City Manufacturing, Inc.,	)	
	)	
Plaintiff,	)	
	)	
vs.	)	Case No. 95-9482
	)	
Scrupulous Corporation,	)	
	)	
Defendant.	)	
	)	

RELEASE OF JUDGMENT

The Plaintiff, _____ Oregon City Manufacturing, Inc. _____, hereby acknowledges that the judgment in this action has been fully satisfied by the Defendant, _____ Scrupulous Corporation _____, and hereby releases and discharges said Defendant from any and all further liability for said judgment.

Dated: _____ October 23, 1998 _____.

Oregon City Manufacturing, Inc.

By: *Harry Truman, IV* _____
Harry Truman, IV, President

SETTLING DISPUTES WITHOUT GOING TO COURT

There's no need to recite horror stories about going to court. It is expensive, slow and chancy. In recent years, various means of *alternative dispute resolution* have become popular. Used correctly, the alternative dispute resolution procedures of *arbitration* or *mediation* can be much more efficient than litigation at settling disputes between parties who can't come to an agreement on their own.

ARBITRATION

An arbitrator is a person who, like an umpire or judge, has the power to decide. The disputants, either by themselves or with the assistance of lawyers, present their arguments to the arbitrator, agreeing in advance to abide by his or her decision. It's a kind of private court system in which the parties get to choose the judge and make their own rules about procedure and evidence.

MEDIATION

A mediator has no power to decide. A mediator is a neutral party who acts as a "go between" to help the parties reach their own compromises and agreements. You might think that a mediator would be useless. If the parties can't agree by themselves, why would they suddenly be able to do so with the help of a mediator who has no power to make decisions? Nevertheless, it frequently works. And it has an advantage over both litigation and arbitration. In court or arbitration, you put the results in the hands of outsiders. Fair decision makers maybe, but still it's like giving them a signed, blank settlement agreement. The judge or arbiter gets to fill in the terms any way he or she wants. In mediation, the only people who can decide are the parties themselves. They keep complete control over the process.

Sample Forms 63 and 64 are clauses to be inserted in a contract by which the parties agree that any disputes to arise will be arbitrated. The first provides for arbitration under the rules of an organization which provides arbitration services. There are many such organizations, the most prominent one being the American Arbitration Association which provides such services around the country. The second provides for arbitrators to be appointed by the parties without being overseen by such an organization.

Sample Form 63. Contract clause for arbitration of disputes; organization rules—

> The parties agree that any controversy, claim or dispute arising out of or related to this agreement or any breach of this agreement shall be submitted to arbitration by and according to the applicable rules of <u>the American Arbitration Association</u> and that judgment upon an award rendered by the arbitrator may be entered in any court having jurisdiction.

Sample Form 64. Contract clause for arbitration of disputes (arbitrator selected by parties)—

> The parties agree that any controversy, claim or dispute arising out of or related to this agreement or any breach of this agreement shall be submitted to arbitration. Such arbitration shall take place in <u>Denver, Colorado</u> or at such other place as may be agreed upon by the parties. The parties shall attempt to agree on one arbitrator. If they are unable to so agree, then each party shall appoint one arbitrator and those appointed shall appoint a third arbitrator. The expenses of arbitration shall be divided equally by the parties. The prevailing party ☐ shall ☒ shall not be entitled to reasonable attorneys' fees. The arbitrators shall conclusively decide all issues of law and fact related to the arbitrated dispute. Judgment upon an award rendered by the arbitrator may be entered in any court having jurisdiction.

Sample Form 65 is to be used after a dispute has arisen and is an agreement to submit the disagreement to arbitration. Sample Form 66 is for mediation. Form 65 provides a fair means of selecting arbitrators. Form 66 presumes that the parties can agree on a mediator, which is usually easy to do since the mediator has no decision making power. Besides, if you can't even agree on a mediator, mediation probably won't be successful. These days there are trained arbitrators, mediators, and arbitration and mediation organizations in most areas. You can locate them through your lawyer or by calling your local or state bar association.

Sample Form 65. **Arbitration agreement—**

ARBITRATION AGREEMENT

This Arbitration Agreement is made this __12th__ day of _____October_____, ___1998___, by and between _____Western Distributors, Inc.,_____and_____Mountain Packaging_____, who agree as follows:

1. The parties agree that any controversy, claim or dispute arising out of or related to:
        the contract executed by and between the parties
        on March 3, 1998.
shall be submitted to arbitration. Such arbitration shall take place at _____
_____7635 Red Rocks Hwy., Denver, CO_____
or at such other place as may be agreed upon by the parties.

2. The parties shall attempt to agree on one arbitrator. If they are unable to so agree, then each party shall appoint one arbitrator and those appointed shall appoint a third arbitrator.

3. The expenses of arbitration shall be divided equally by the parties.

4. The arbitrators shall conclusively decide all issues of law and fact related to the arbitrated dispute. Judgment upon an award rendered by the arbitrator may be entered in any court having jurisdiction.

5. The prevailing party ☐ shall ☒ shall not be entitled to reasonable attorneys' fees.

Western Distributors, Inc.   Mountain Packaging, a general
                                          partnership

Wanda Miller   *Marilyn Kim*
Wanda Miller, President   Marilyn Kim, general partner

Attest: *Martin Miller*
Martin Miller, Secretary

Sample Form 66. Mediation agreement—

MEDIATION AGREEMENT

The undersigned parties are engaged in a dispute regarding <u>the contract</u> <u>between the parties dated February 12, 1998</u>. We hereby agree to submit such dispute to mediation by <u>Neighborhood Mediation Services</u> and that all matters resolved in mediation shall be reduced to a binding written agreement signed by the parties. The costs of mediation shall be borne equally by the parties.

Dated: <u>August 8, 1998</u>.

Scrupulous Corporation

Marketing Associates,
a general partnership

Henry Hardy

Murray Madison

Henry Hardy, President

Murray Madison,
general partner

MISCELLANEOUS FORMS 10

UNSOLICITED IDEAS, PROPOSALS, AND MATERIALS

You may be contacted by individuals who offer ideas, proposals, or materials to help your business. These might include such things as marketing concepts, new products, or ideas to improve existing products. Such unsolicited offers can pose a problem if you are already considering something similar. If you reject the offer, and then come out with something similar, you may find yourself charged with stealing the idea. Sample Form 67 is an example of a form that can be used to try to give yourself some protection. (See Form 16 in the appendix.)

Sample Form 67. Response to submission of unsolicited idea—

FROM:	Scrupulous Corporation 400 West 61st Avenue P.O. Box 19 New York, NY 10032	DATE: July 9, 1998
TO:	William Jackson 2204 East River Place, #19A New York, NY 10030	

Dear   Mr. Jackson:

Thank you for your interest in our company in submitting your material for our review. We receive many ideas, proposals, and other materials, and also have many of our own projects under consideration and development. Therefore, it is possible that what is contained in your submission is already under planning or development, or has previously been considered.

❑ It is our company policy not to accept unsolicited ideas, proposals, or materials, therefore, we are returning your material unopened.

❑ It is our company policy not to accept unsolicited ideas, proposals, or materials, therefore, we are returning your material. Although we prefer to return such materials unopened, it was impossible to know that your package was such a submission until it was opened.

☒ If you would like us to consider your material, you will need to submit it along with an executed and witnessed copy of this form, agreeing to the following terms and conditions:

1. We do not accept any responsibility for loss of the materials your submit, or for keeping your submission confidential, although we will use our best efforts to keep it confidential.

2. Your submission will be returned to you only if you prepay return postage or freight.

3. We agree that this document does not give us any rights in your submission, and we will not exploit your idea, proposal or material in any way without first entering into an agreement for compensation.

4. We will only pay compensation if all of the following applies: a) we accept your idea, proposal or material, b) we have received the idea, proposal or material only from you [i.e., we will have no obligation to you if your idea, proposal, or material is currently under consideration, planning or development by us], and c) we enter into a written agreement with you as to the terms and conditions for use of your idea, proposal or material and the compensation to be paid to you.

Henry Hardy
‾‾‾‾‾‾‾‾‾‾‾‾‾‾‾‾‾‾‾‾‾‾‾‾‾‾‾‾‾‾‾‾‾‾‾‾
Henry Hardy, President

I understand and agree to the foregoing terms and conditions.

Dated:_____

_____   _____
Witness   Submitter

QUOTES AND ENDORSEMENTS

There may be times when you will want to use a quote, photograph, endorsement or other material of someone else for advertising purposes.

This will require you to obtain the person's written permission. Form 17 in the appendix is to use for obtaining such permission. Sample Form 68 is an example of this form as you would fill it in before giving it to the person for his or her signature, and the signature of a witness.

Sample Form 68. Permission to use quote, personal statement, or other material—

PERMISSION TO USE QUOTE, PERSONAL STATEMENT, OR OTHER MATERIAL

The undersigned hereby authorizes _____ Scrupulous Corporation _____
_____, its successors and assigns, to use, publish, print and otherwise communicate, in whole or in part, the following statement, endorsement, quotation, photograph, or other material attached described as:

Black and white photograph of the undersigned with the following endorsement: "I use Scrupulous products whenever they are available, and I've never been disappointed."

Quote may be used either with or without photograph.

☒ see copy attached hereto.

This authorization ☐ is ☒ is not exclusive.

This authorization ☐ is unlimited ☒ is limited as follows:

This authorization is only for the period through December 31, 1999. Use is limited to advertisements in magazine, catalogs, and other written advertisements, but not on television or radio.

The undersigned acknowledges that this authorization is nonrevocable, and that no other or further payment or consideration is due.

Signed on _____.

_____   _____
Witness   Signature

Name:_____   Name:_____
Address:_____   Address:_____
_____   _____

AFFIDAVITS

If you want someone to make a written statement swearing that one thing or another is true, a useful tool is the affidavit. Sample Form 69 is drafted for use by a corporate officer, but it can be easily altered for use by a person in an individual capacity by deleting references to the corporation. (For certifications of various corporate resolutions and minutes, see *The Most Valuable Corporate Forms You'll Ever Need*.)

Sample Form 69. General affidavit—

AFFIDAVIT

The undersigned, being first duly sworn, deposes and says:

1. I am the duly appointed personnel director of Scrupulous Corporation, I keep and maintain all personnel records of present and past employees of Scrupulous Corporation, and I am personally acquainted with Paula T. Harper.

2. According to the personnel records of Scrupulous Corporation, Paula T. Harper, Social Security Number 555-55-5555, became employed by Scrupulous Corporation as Manager of Accounts Receivable, on October 1, 1988, and has been so employed continuously since that date.

3. Ms. Harper's initial rate of pay was $15,000 per year, and her current rate of pay is $23,000 per year.

4. Based upon the needs of Scrupulous Corporation, and Ms. Harper's excellent employment record, her continued employment and chances for advancement are excellent.

This affidavit was executed by me on ___December 16, 1998___.

Sharon MacGregor
Sharon MacGregor

[Notary public acknowledgment omitted to save space]

RECEIPTS

A receipt is nothing more than acknowledgment that something was left in the possession of the person signing the receipt. Form 47 in the appendix includes a receipt for money, and a receipt for other forms of property.

Appendix

Forms

The forms in this appendix are blank forms for you to use. It is suggested that you photocopy the forms for use, leaving those in the book to photocopy again for future use. These forms can also be modified to fit your specific needs. The forms in the appendix are not in any particular order.

Lines are provided for signatures. The signature format will vary depending upon whether it is an individual, partnership, or corporation that is signing. There may be more lines than you need on the forms. If so, just ignore the extra lines. Be sure to add the notation "(Seal)" after an individual's signature or the signature of a partner who is signing for a partnership. If the person is signing for a partnership or corporation, you will need to type in the name of the partnership or corporation several lines above the signature line, add the word "By" on the signature line, and type in the signer's name and title just below the signature line. If the corporate secretary or assistant secretary is attesting to the signature of the office, you will need to add the word "Attest:" to the appropriate signature line, and type in the person's name and title just below that signature line. For more information to help you determine the proper signature format, refer to the section in chapter 1 on "Signatures."

The requirements for notary public acknowledgments varies from state to state. Some states just require a simple statement that the person signed before the notary, some require the notary to see some form of identification and to keep a record, and others require the document itself to state what form of identification was produced. For the forms in this book, a more detailed format was used. It may exceed what is required in your state, or something may need to be changed or added. The notary in your state should know the requirements, and can modify the form if necessary to comply with legal requirements.

TABLE OF FORMS

CONTRACT

THIS AGREEMENT is entered into by and between _____ _____ (hereafter referred to as _____) and _____ (hereafter referred to as _____). In consideration of the mutual promises made in this agreement and other valuable consideration, the receipt and sufficiency of which is acknowledged, the parties agree as follows:

Page 1 of _____ pages.

The following addenda, dated the same date as this agreement, are incorporated in, and made a part of, this agreement:

❏ None.

This agreement shall be governed by the laws of _____.

If any part of this agreement is adjudged invalid, illegal, or unenforceable, the remaining parts shall not be affected and shall remain in full force and effect.

This agreement shall be binding upon the parties, and upon their heirs, executors, personal representatives, administrators, and assigns. No person shall have a right or cause of action arising out of or resulting from this agreement except those who are parties to it and their successors in interest.

This instrument, including any attached exhibits and addenda, constitutes the entire agreement of the parties. No representations or promises have been made except those that are set out in this agreement. This agreement may not be modified except in writing signed by all the parties.

IN WITNESS WHEREOF the parties have signed this agreement under seal on _____.

_____   _____

_____   _____

Page _____ of _____ pages.

ADDENDUM TO CONTRACT

Addendum No. _____

    The following terms are a part of the Contract, dated _____, by and between _____ and
_____ :

_____   _____

_____   _____

AMENDMENT TO CONTRACT

For valuable consideration, the receipt and sufficiency of which is acknowledged by each of the parties, this agreement amends a Contract dated _____, between _____ and _____ , relating to _____ . This contract amendment is hereby incorporated into the Contract.

Except as changed by this amendment, the Contract shall continue in effect according to its terms. The amendments herein shall be effective on the date this document is executed by all parties.

IN WITNESS WHEREOF the parties have signed this agreement under seal on

_____ .

_____   _____

_____   _____

Assignment of Contract

FOR VALUE RECEIVED the undersigned (the "Assignor") hereby assigns, transfers, and conveys to _____ (the "Assignee") all the Assignor's rights, title and interests in and to a contract (the "Contract") dated _____, between _____ and _____.

The Assignor hereby warrants and represents that the Contract is in full force and effect and is fully assignable.

The Assignee hereby assumes the duties and obligations of the Assignor under the Contract and agrees to hold the Assignor harmless from any claim or demand thereunder.

The date of this assignment is _____.

IN WITNESS WHEREOF the parties have signed this agreement under seal on _____.

Assignor: Assignee:

_____   _____

_____   _____

APPLICATION FOR EMPLOYMENT

We consider applicants for all positions without regard to race, color, religion, sex, national origin, age, marital or veteran status, the presence of a non-job-related medical condition or handicap, or any other legally protected status. Proof of citizenship or immigration status will be required upon employment.

(PLEASE TYPE OR PRINT)

Position Applied For   Date of Application

Last Name	First Name	Middle Name or Initial

Address	*Number Street*	*City*	*State*	*Zip Code*

Telephone Number(s) [indicate home or work]	Social Security Number

Date Available:_____   Are you available: ☐ Full Time   ☐ Part Time   ☐ Weekends

Have you been convicted of a felony within the past 7 years?   ☐ Yes   ☐ No
    Conviction will not necessarily disqualify an applicant from employment.
If Yes, attach explanation.

Education

	High School	Undergraduate	Graduate
School Name & Location			
Years Completed	1 2 3 4	1 2 3 4	1 2 3 4
Diploma / Degree			
Course of Study			

State any additional information you feel may be helpful to us in considering your application (such as any specialized training; skills; apprenticeships; honors received; professional, trade, business or civic organizations or activities; job-related military training or experience; foreign language abilities; etc.)

_____
_____
_____
_____

Employment Experience

Start with your present or last job. Include any job-related military service assignments and voluntary activities. You may exclude organizations which indicate race, color, religion, gender, national origin, handicap, or other protected status.

1.

Employer Name & Address	Dates Employed	Job Title/Duties
	Hourly Rate/Salary	
May we contact this employer? ☐ Yes ☐ No	Hours Per Week	
Employer Phone		
Supervisor		
Reason for Leaving		

2.

Employer Name & Address	Dates Employed	Job Title/Duties
	Hourly Rate/Salary	
Employer Phone	Hours Per Week	
Supervisor		
Reason for Leaving		

3.

Employer Name & Address	Dates Employed	Job Title/Duties
	Hourly Rate/Salary	
Employer Phone	Hours Per Week	
Supervisor		
Reason for Leaving		

4.

Employer Name & Address	Dates Employed	Job Title/Duties
	Hourly Rate/Salary	
Employer Phone	Hours Per Week	
Supervisor		
Reason for Leaving		

If you need additional space, continue on a separate sheet of paper.

Applicant's Statement

I certify that the information given on this application is true and complete to the best of my knowledge. I authorize investigation of all statements contained in this application, and understand that false or misleading information given in my application or interview(s) may result in discharge.

I understand and acknowledge that, unless otherwise defined by applicable law, any employment relationship with this organization is "at will," which means that I may resign at any time and the employer may discharge me at any time with or without cause. I further understand that this "at will" employment relationship may not be changed orally, by any written document, or by conduct, unless such change is specifically acknowledged in writing by an authorized executive of this organization.

_____   _____

Signature of Applicant   Date

EMPLOYMENT AGREEMENT

This employment agreement is entered into by and between _____

_____(the "Employee") and _____

_____ (the "Employer"), who agree as follows:

1. The Employer has hired the Employee to fill the following position:

❑ See attached description.

2. Term. The term of Employee's employment shall begin on _____.
Employment pursuant to this agreement shall be "at will" and may be ended by the Employee or by the Employer at any time and for any reason. This is an agreement for employment that is:

❑ permanent, but "at will."

❑ temporary, but "at will," _____

_____.

3. Probation. It is understood that the first _____ days of employment shall be probationary only and that if the Employee's services are not satisfactory to the Employer employment shall be terminated at the end of this probationary period.

4. Compensation and Benefits. The Employee's compensation and benefits during the term of this agreement shall be as stated in this paragraph, and may be adjusted from time to time by the Employer. Initially, the Employer shall pay the Employee:

❑ a salary in the amount of _____, payable

_____.

❑ an hourly wage of $_____ , payable _____.

❑ a commission of _____% of _____.

In addition to such commission, the Employee shall receive _____

_____.

❑ the following benefits: _____

_____.

❑ other:

5. Work Hours. The hours and schedule worked by the Employee may be adjusted from time to time by the Employer. Initially, the Employee shall work the following hours each week:

6.   Additional Terms. The Employee also agrees to the terms of the attached:

❑ No other agreements are attached   ❑ Confidentiality Agreement

❑ Agreement on Patents and Inventions   ❑ Indemnification Agreement

❑ Other:_____

7.   This agreement shall be governed by the laws of _____.

8.   It is the Employer's intention to comply with all federal, state and local laws which apply to the business, including but not limited to labor, equal opportunity, privacy and sexual harassment laws. The Employee shall promptly report to the Employer any violations encountered in the business. The Employee shall at all time comply with any and all federal, state and local laws.

9.   The Employee shall not have the power to make any contracts or commitments on behalf of the Employer without the express written consent of the Employer.

10. In the event one party fails to insist upon performance of a part of this agreement, such failure shall not be construed as waiving those terms, and this entire agreement shall remain in full force.

11. In the event a dispute of any nature arises between the parties to this agreement, the parties agree to submit the dispute to binding arbitration under the rules of the American Arbitration Association. An award rendered by the arbitrator(s) shall be final and binding upon the parties and judgment on such award may be entered by either party in the highest court having jurisdiction. Each party specifically waives his or her right to bring the dispute before a court of law and stipulates that this agreement shall be a complete defense to any action instituted in any local, state or federal court or before any administrative tribunal.

12. If any part of this agreement is adjudged invalid, illegal, or unenforceable, the remaining parts shall not be affected and shall remain in full force and effect.

13. This agreement shall be binding upon the parties, and upon their heirs, executors, personal representatives, administrators, and assigns. No person shall have a right or cause of action arising out of or resulting from this agreement except those who are parties to it and their successors in interest.

14. This is instrument, including any attached agreements specified in paragraph 5 above, constitutes the entire agreement of the parties. No representations or promises have been made except those that are set out in this agreement. This agreement may not be modified except in writing signed by all the parties.

15. IN WITNESS WHEREOF the parties have signed this agreement under seal on

_____.

Employer: Employee:

_____   _____

_____   _____

CONFIDENTIALITY AGREEMENT

This agreement is made between _____ (the "Employee") and _____ (the "Employer"). The Employee agrees to the terms of this agreement:

❏ as part of the terms of the Employee being hired by the Employer.

❏ in consideration of the Employee's continued employment by the Employer and additional consideration consisting of _____, which the Employee acknowledges is sufficient consideration paid by the Employer over and above the consideration due to the Employee pursuant to his or her usual terms of employment.

1. The Employee acknowledges that, in the course of employment by the Employer, the Employee has, and may in the future, come into the possession of certain confidential information belonging to the Employer including but not limited to trade secrets, customer lists, supplier lists and prices, pricing schedules, methods, processes, or marketing plans.

2. The Employee hereby covenants and agrees that he or she will at no time, during or after the term of employment, use for his or her own benefit or the benefit of others, or disclose or divulge to others, any such confidential information.

3. Upon termination of employment, the Employee will return to the Employer, retaining no copies, all documents relating to the Employer's business including, but not limited to, reports, manuals, drawings, diagrams, blueprints, correspondence, customer lists, computer programs, and all other materials and all copies of such materials, obtained by the Employee during employment.

4. Violation of this agreement by the Employee will entitle the Employer to an injunction to prevent such competition or disclosure (posting of any bond by the Employer is hereby waived), and will entitle the Employer to other legal remedies, including attorneys' fees and costs.

5. This agreement shall be governed by the laws of _____.

6. If any part of this agreement is adjudged invalid, illegal, or unenforceable, the remaining parts shall not be affected and shall remain in full force and effect.

7. This agreement shall be binding upon the parties, and upon their heirs, executors, personal representatives, administrators, and assigns. No person shall have a right or cause of action arising out of or resulting from this agreement except those who are parties to it and their successors in interest.

8. This instrument, including any attached exhibits and addenda, constitutes the entire agreement of the parties. No representations or promises have been made except those that are set out in this agreement. This agreement may not be modified except in writing signed by all the parties.

IN WITNESS WHEREOF the parties have signed this agreement under seal on _____.

Employer: Employee:

_____   _____

_____   _____

AGREEMENT ON PATENTS AND INVENTIONS

This agreement is made between _____ (the "Employee") and _____ (the "Employer"). The Employee agrees to the terms of this agreement:

❑ as part of the terms of the Employee being hired by the Employer.

❑ in consideration of the Employee's continued employment by the Employer and additional consideration consisting of _____, which the Employee acknowledges is sufficient consideration paid by the Employer over and above the consideration due to the Employee pursuant to his or her usual terms of employment.

1. During the term of the Employee's employment and for a period of _____ months thereafter, the Employee will promptly and completely disclose and assign to the Employer every invention, product, process, mechanism or design that the Employee may invent, create, develop or discover which in any way relates to, or may be suggested by, the Employer's business or the Employee's employment duties. Such disclosure or assignment shall be made free of any obligation by the Employer to the Employee and without the necessity of any further request by the Employer.

2. The Employee will, at the Employer's expense, cooperate with the Employer in applying for and securing in the name of the Employer patents with respect to the matters required to be disclosed pursuant to this agreement in each country where the Employer wishes to secure such patents. Without limiting the foregoing, the Employee will promptly execute all proper documents presented to him or her for signature by the Employer in connection with the securing of such patents and the transfer of such patents to the Employer and will give such true information and testimony, under oath if so requested, as the Employer may reasonably require in connection with such matters.

3. The following is a complete list of all inventions, applications for patent, and patents in which the Employee holds an interest, and which are not subject to this agreement:

4. This agreement shall be governed by the laws of _____.

5. If any part of this agreement is adjudged invalid, illegal, or unenforceable, the remaining parts shall not be affected and shall remain in full force and effect.

6. This agreement shall be binding upon the parties, and upon their heirs, executors, personal representatives, administrators, and assigns. No person shall have a right or cause of action arising out of or resulting from this agreement except those who are parties to it and their successors in interest.

7. This instrument, including any attached exhibits and addenda, constitutes the entire agreement of the parties. No representations or promises have been made except those that are set out in this agreement. This agreement may not be modified except in writing signed by all the parties.

IN WITNESS WHEREOF the parties have signed this agreement under seal on _____.

Employer: Employee:

_____   _____

_____   _____

NON-COMPETITION AGREEMENT

This agreement is made between _____ (the "Employee") and _____ (the "Employer"). The Employee agrees to the terms of this agreement:

❑ as part of the terms of the Employee being initially hired by the Employer.

❑ in consideration of the Employee's continued employment by the Employer and additional consideration consisting of _____, which the Employee acknowledges is sufficient consideration paid by the Employer over and above the consideration due to the Employee pursuant to his or her usual terms of employment.

1. The Employee agrees that he or she will not compete, directly or indirectly, as a business owner, partner, corporation, employee, agent or otherwise, with the business of the Employer or any of the Employer's successors or assigns.

2. "Not compete," as used herein, shall mean that the Employee, directly or indirectly, as an owner, partner, officer, director, stockholder, employee, consultant, agent or otherwise (except as a passive investment stockholder in a publicly owned corporation), shall not engage in any business or activity described as: _____,

3. This agreement shall apply to such business or activity within the following geographical area: _____, and shall remain in full force and effect for a period of _____.

4. In the event of any breach of this agreement by the Employee, the Employer shall be entitled to injunctive relief without posting any bond, in addition to any other legal rights and remedies.

5. This agreement shall be governed by the laws of _____.

6. If any part of this agreement is adjudged invalid, illegal, or unenforceable, the remaining parts shall not be affected and shall remain in full force and effect.

7. This agreement shall be binding upon the parties, and upon their heirs, executors, personal representatives, administrators, and assigns. No person shall have a right or cause of action arising out of or resulting from this agreement except those who are parties to it and their successors in interest.

8. This instrument, including any attached exhibits and addenda, constitutes the entire agreement of the parties. No representations or promises have been made except those that are set out in this agreement. This agreement may not be modified except in writing signed by all the parties.

IN WITNESS WHEREOF the parties have signed this agreement under seal on _____.

Employer: Employee:

_____   _____

_____   _____

APPOINTMENT OF SALES REPRESENTATIVE

This agreement is entered into by and between _____
(the "Agent") and _____
(the "Company"). It is agreed by the Agent and the Company as follows:

1.   The Company has appointed the Agent as its representative for the sale of _____
_____in the following territory:
_____.
The territory may be changed from time to time upon agreement by the Company and the Agent.
The Agent agrees to use his or her best efforts in the sale of such in the territory assigned.

2.   The term of Agent's appointment shall begin on _____, and
may be ended by the Agent or by the Company at any time and for any reason.

3.   All sales made by the Agent shall be at prices and terms set by the Company, and no sales
contracts shall be valid until accepted by a duly authorized officer of the Company.

4.   The Agent's compensation and benefits during the term of this agreement shall be as stated
in this paragraph, and may be adjusted from time to time by the Company. The Company shall pay
the Agent a commission of _____% based on the net selling price of the goods actually received by
the Company. In the event part or all of the purchase price is refunded to the purchaser for any reason, the Agent's commission based on such amounts refunded shall be returned by the Agent to the
Company or deducted by the Company from the Agent's future commissions. The Company shall
not be liable to the Agent for commissions on orders unfilled by the Company for any reason. In addition to the commissions provided for in this agreement, the Agent shall receive _____
_____.

5.   The Company shall reimburse the Agent for expenses according to a schedule published
from time to time by the Company.

6.   The parties agree that no employer - employee relationship is created by this agreement, but
the relationship of the Agent to the Company shall be that of an independent contractor.

7.   This agreement shall be governed by the laws of _____.
If any part of this agreement is adjudged invalid, illegal, or unenforceable, the remaining parts shall
not be affected and shall remain in full force and effect. This agreement shall be binding upon the
parties, and upon their heirs, executors, personal representatives, administrators, and assigns. No person shall have a right or cause of action arising out of or resulting from this agreement except those
who are parties to it and their successors in interest.

8.   This instrument, including any attached exhibits and addenda, constitutes the entire agreement of the parties. No representations or promises have been made except those that are set out in
this agreement. This agreement may not be modified except in writing signed by all the parties.

IN WITNESS WHEREOF the parties have signed this agreement under seal on
_____.

Company: Agent:

_____   _____

_____   _____

INDEMNIFICATION AGREEMENT

In exchange for _____ and other valuable consideration, the receipt and sufficiency of which is hereby acknowledged, the undersigned hereby agrees to indemnify and hold _____ (the "Company") harmless from any claim, action, liability or suit arising out of or in any way connected with the following:

In the event any claim reasonably believed by the Company to be subject to indemnification under this agreement is asserted against the Company, the Company will provide timely notice of such claim to the undersigned. The undersigned will thereafter, at its own expense, defend and protect the Company against such claim. Should the undersigned be unable or fail to so defend the Company, the Company shall have the right to defend or settle such claim, and the undersigned shall reimburse the Company for all settlements, judgments, fees, costs, expenses and payments, including reasonable attorneys' fees, incurred by the Company in connection with the discharge of such claim.

This agreement shall be governed by the laws of _____.

If any part of this agreement is adjudged invalid, illegal, or unenforceable, the remaining parts shall not be affected and shall remain in full force and effect.

This agreement shall be binding upon the parties, and upon their heirs, executors, personal representatives, administrators, and assigns. No person shall have a right or cause of action arising out of or resulting from this agreement except those who are parties to it and their successors in interest.

This instrument, including any attached exhibits and addenda, constitutes the entire agreement of the parties. No representations or promises have been made except those that are set out in this agreement. This agreement may not be modified except in writing signed by all the parties.

IN WITNESS WHEREOF the parties have signed this agreement under seal on _____.

_____   _____

_____   _____

117

WORK MADE-FOR-HIRE AGREEMENT

This Agreement is made this _____ day of _____, _____, between _____ as Owner, and _____as Author/Artist.

WHEREAS the Owner wishes to commission a Work called _____ _____ and;

WHEREAS the Author/Artist has represented that he/she can create said work according to the specifications provided by the Owner;

It is agreed between the parties hereto that in consideration of the sum of $_____, to be paid by the Owner to the Author/Artist within 30 days of satisfactory completion of the work, the Author/Artist shall create the Work as specified. Upon payment, the Owner shall acquire all rights to the commissioned Work including copyright.

The Author/Artist warrants that the Work will be original and will not infringe or plagiarize any other work; will not libel any person or invade any person's right to privacy; and will not contain any unlawful materials. The Author/Artist shall indemnify and save the Owner harmless from any loss or liability due to any breach of these warranties, including reasonable attorneys fees.

The Author/Artist shall be responsible for all costs in creation of the Work unless otherwise agreed to in writing by the Owner.

This agreement shall be governed by the laws of _____.

If any part of this agreement is adjudged invalid, illegal, or unenforceable, the remaining parts shall not be affected and shall remain in full force and effect.

This agreement shall be binding upon the parties, and upon their heirs, executors, personal representatives, administrators, and assigns. No person shall have a right or cause of action arising out of or resulting from this agreement except those who are parties to it and their successors in interest.

This instrument, including any attached exhibits and addenda, constitutes the entire agreement of the parties. No representations or promises have been made except those that are set out in this agreement. This agreement may not be modified except in writing signed by all the parties.

IN WITNESS WHEREOF the parties have signed this agreement under seal on _____.

Owner: Author/Artist:

_____   _____

_____   _____

INDEPENDENT CONTRACTOR AGREEMENT

This indemnification agreement is entered into by and between _____ _____ (the "Company") and _____ _____ (the "Contractor"). It is agreed by the parties as follows:

1. The Contractor shall supply all of the labor and materials to perform the following work for the Company as an independent contractor:

❏ The attached plans and specifications are to be followed and are hereby made a part of this Agreement.

2. The Contractor agrees to the following completion dates for portions of the work and final completion of the work:

<u>Description of Work</u>   <u>Completion Date</u>

3. The Contractor shall perform the work in a workman-like manner, according to standard industry practices, unless other standards or requirements are set forth in any attached plans and specifications.

4. The Company shall pay the Contractor the sum of $_____, in full payment for the work as set forth in this Agreement, to be paid as follows:

5. Any additional work or services shall be agreed to in writing, signed by both parties.

6. The Contractor shall obtain and maintain any licenses or permits necessary for the work to be performed. The Contractor shall obtain and maintain any required insurance, including but not limited to workers' compensation insurance, to cover the Contractor's employees and agents.

7. The Contractor shall be responsible for the payment of any sub-contractors and shall obtain lien releases from sub-contractors as may be necessary. The Contractor agrees to indemnify and hold harmless the Company from any claims or liability arising out of the work performed by the Contractor under this Agreement.

8. Time is of the essence of this Agreement.

9. This instrument, including any attached exhibits and addenda, constitutes the entire agreement of the parties. No representations or promises have been made except those that are set out in this agreement. This agreement may not be modified except in writing signed by all the parties.

10. This agreement shall be governed by the laws of _____.

11. If any part of this agreement is adjudged invalid, illegal, or unenforceable, the remaining parts shall not be affected and shall remain in full force and effect.

12. This agreement shall be binding upon the parties, and upon their heirs, executors, personal representatives, administrators, and assigns. No person shall have a right or cause of action arising out of or resulting from this agreement except those who are parties to it and their successors in interest.

13. This instrument, including any attached exhibits and addenda, constitutes the entire agreement of the parties. No representations or promises have been made except those that are set out in this agreement. This agreement may not be modified except in writing signed by all the parties.

IN WITNESS WHEREOF the parties have signed this agreement under seal on _____.

Company: Contractor:

_____   _____

_____   _____

ASSIGNMENT OF COPYRIGHT

This Assignment is made this _____ day of _____, _____, between _____ as Owner of the copyright on the Work known as _____

_____

_____,

and _____ as Purchaser.

WHEREAS the Owner is sole owner of all rights in the Work and whereas the Purchaser is desirous of purchasing all such rights,

IT IS AGREED between the parties hereto that in consideration of the sum of $_____, the receipt of which is hereby acknowledged, the Owner hereby assigns to the Purchaser all of his/her interest in the Work and the copyright thereon, which interest shall be held for the full term of said copyright.

IN WITNESS WHEREOF, the Owner has executed this Agreement on the date above written.

_____

STATE OF   )
COUNTY OF   )

I certify that _____ ,who ❏ is personally known to me to be the person whose name is subscribed to the foregoing instrument ❏ produced _____ as identification, personally appeared before me on _____, and ❏ acknowledged the execution of the foregoing instrument ❏ acknowledged that (s)he is (Assistant) Secretary of _____ _____and that by authority duly given and as the act of the corporation, the foregoing instrument was signed in its name by its (Vice) President, sealed with its corporate seal and attested by him/her as its (Assistant) Secretary.

_____
Notary Public, State of

Notary's commission expires:

COPYRIGHT LICENSE

This License is made this _____ day of _____, _____.
between _____
as Owner of the copyright on the Work known as _____
_____ and _____ as Licensee.

WHEREAS the Owner is sole owner of all rights in the Work and whereas the Licensee is desirous of purchasing rights in said Work;

IT IS AGREED between the parties hereto that in consideration of the sum of $_____, the receipt of which is hereby acknowledged, the Owner hereby licenses the License to use the copyrighted Work as follows:

It is understood between the parties that this License covers only those uses listed above for the time period stated. All other rights in and to the copyrighted work shall remain the property of the Owner.

This agreement shall be governed by the laws of _____.

If any part of this agreement is adjudged invalid, illegal, or unenforceable, the remaining parts shall not be affected and shall remain in full force and effect.

This agreement shall be binding upon the parties, and upon their heirs, executors, personal representatives, administrators, and assigns. No person shall have a right or cause of action arising out of or resulting from this agreement except those who are parties to it and their successors in interest.

This instrument, including any attached exhibits and addenda, constitutes the entire agreement of the parties. No representations or promises have been made except those that are set out in this agreement. This agreement may not be modified except in writing signed by all the parties.

IN WITNESS WHEREOF the parties have signed this agreement under seal on _____.

Owner: Licensee:

_____   _____

_____   _____

FROM:

TO:

Dear

Thank you for your interest in our company in submitting your material for our review. We receive many ideas, proposals, and other materials, and also have many of our own projects under consideration and development. Therefore, it is possible that what is contained in your submission is already under planning or development, or has previously been considered.

❏ It is our company policy not to accept unsolicited ideas, proposals, or materials, therefore, we are returning your material unopened.

❏ It is our company policy not to accept unsolicited ideas, proposals, or materials, therefore, we are returning your material. Although we prefer to return such materials unopened, it was impossible to know that your package was such a submission until it was opened.

❏ If you would like us to consider your material, you will need to submit it along with an executed and witnessed copy of this form, agreeing to the following terms and conditions:

1. We do not accept any responsibility for loss of the materials you submit, or for keeping your submission confidential, although we will use our best efforts to keep it confidential.

2. Your submission will be returned to you only if you prepay return postage or freight.

3. We agree that this document does not give us any rights in your submission, and we will not exploit your idea, proposal or material in any way without first entering into an agreement for compensation.

4. We will only pay compensation if all of the following applies: a) we accept your idea, proposal or material, b) we have received the idea, proposal or material only from you [i.e., we will have no obligation to you if your idea, proposal, or material is currently under consideration, planning or development by us], and c) we enter into a written agreement with you as to the terms and conditions for use of your idea, proposal or material and the compensation to be paid to you.

_____

I understand and agree to the foregoing terms and conditions.

Dated:_____

_____   _____
Witness   Submitter

PERMISSION TO USE QUOTE, PERSONAL STATEMENT, OR OTHER MATERIAL

The undersigned hereby authorizes _____
_____, its successors and assigns, to use, publish, print and otherwise communicate, in whole or in part, the following statement, endorsement, quotation, photograph, or other material attached described as:

❏ see copy attached hereto.

This authorization   ❏ is   ❏ is not   exclusive.

This authorization   ❏ is unlimited   ❏ is limited as follows:

The undersigned acknowledges that this authorization is nonrevocable, and that no other or further payment or consideration is due.

Signed on _____.

_____
Witness

Name:_____
Address:_____
_____

_____
Signature

Name:_____
Address:_____
_____

U.S. Department of Justice
Immigration and Naturalization Service

OMB No. 1115-0136 *Form 18*
Employment Eligibility Verification

Please read instructions carefully before completing this form. The instructions must be available during completion of this form. **ANTI-DISCRIMINATION NOTICE.** It is illegal to discriminate against work eligible individuals. Employers CANNOT specify which document(s) they will accept from an employee. The refusal to hire an individual because of a future expiration date may also constitute illegal discrimination.

Section 1. Employee Information and Verification. To be completed and signed by employee at the time employment begins

Print Name: Last	First	Middle Initial	Maiden Name

Address (Street Name and Number)	Apt. #	Date of Birth (month/day/year)

City	State	Zip Code	Social Security #

I am aware that federal law provides for imprisonment and/or fines for false statements or use of false documents in connection with the completion of this form.

I attest, under penalty of perjury, that I am (check one of the following):
- ☐ A citizen or national of the United States
- ☐ A Lawful Permanent Resident (Alien # A_____)
- ☐ An alien authorized to work until ____/____/____
  (Alien # or Admission #_____)

Employee's Signature	Date (month/day/year)

Preparer and/or Translator Certification. *(To be completed and signed if Section 1 is prepared by a person other than the employee.) I attest, under penalty of perjury, that I have assisted in the completion of this form and that to the best of my knowledge the information is true and correct.*

Preparer's/Translator's Signature	Print Name

Address (Street Name and Number, City, State, Zip Code)	Date (month/day/year)

Section 2. Employer Review and Verification. To be completed and signed by employer. **Examine one document from List A OR examine one document from List B and one from List C** as listed on the reverse of this form and record the title, number and expiration date, if any, of the document(s)

List A	OR	List B	AND	List C
Document title: _____		_____		_____
Issuing authority: _____		_____		_____
Document #: _____		_____		_____
Expiration Date (if any): ___/___/___		___/___/___		___/___/___
Document #: _____				
Expiration Date (if any): ___/___/___				

CERTIFICATION - I attest, under penalty of perjury, that I have examined the document(s) presented by the above-named employee, that the above-listed document(s) appear to be genuine and to relate to the employee named, that the employee began employment on (month/day/year) ___/___/___ **and that to the best of my knowledge the employee is eligible to work in the United States. (State employment agencies may omit the date the employee began employment).**

Signature of Employer or Authorized Representative	Print Name	Title

Business or Organization Name	Address (Street Name and Number, City, State, Zip Code)	Date (month/day/year)

Section 3. Updating and Reverification. To be completed and signed by employer

New Name (if applicable)	B. Date of rehire (month/day/year) (if applicable)

If employee's previous grant of work authorization has expired, provide the information below for the document that establishes current employment eligibility.

Document Title:_____ Document #:_____ Expiration Date (if any):___/___/___

I attest, under penalty of perjury, that to the best of my knowledge, this employee is eligible to work in the United States, and if the employee presented document(s), the document(s) I have examined appear to be genuine and to relate to the individual.

Signature of Employer or Authorized Representative	Date (month/day/year)

INSTRUCTIONS
PLEASE READ ALL INSTRUCTIONS CAREFULLY BEFORE COMPLETING THIS FORM.

Anti-Discrimination Notice. It is illegal to discriminate against any individual (other than an alien not authorized to work in U.S.) in hiring, discharging, or recruiting or referring for a fee because of that individual's national origin or citizenship status. I illegal to discriminate against work eligible individuals. Employers **CANNOT** specify which document(s) they will accept from employee. The refusal to hire an individual because of a future expiration date may also constitute illegal discrimination.

Section 1 - Employee. All employees, citizens and noncitizens, hired after November 6, 1986, must complete Section 1 of this form at the time of hire, which is the actual beginning of employment. **The employer is responsible for ensuring that Section 1 is timely and properly completed.**

Preparer/Translator Certification. The Preparer/Translator Certification must be completed if Section 1 is prepared by a person other than the employee. A preparer/translator may be used only when the employee is unable to complete Section 1 on his/her own. However, the employee must still sign Section 1 personally.

Section 2 - Employer. For the purpose of completing this form, the term "employer" includes those recruiters and referrers for a fee who are agricultural associations, agricultural employers, or farm labor contractors.

Employers must complete Section 2 by examining evidence of identity and employment eligibility within three (3) business days of the date employment begins. If employees are authorized to work, but are unable to present the required document(s) within three business days, they must present a receipt for the application of the document(s) within three business days and the actual document(s) within ninety (90) days. However, if employers hire individuals for a duration of less than three business days, Section 2 must be completed at the time employment begins. **Employers must record: 1)** document title; **2)** issuing authority; **3)** document number, **4)** expiration date, if any; and **5)** the date employment begins. Employers must sign and date the certification. Employees must present original documents. Employers may, but are not required to, photocopy the document(s) presented. These photocopies may only be used for the verification process and must be retained with the I-9. **However, employers are still responsible for completing the I-9.**

Section 3 - Updating and Reverification. Employers must complete Section 3 when updating and/or reverifying the I-9. Employers must reverify employment eligibility of their employees on or before the expiration date recorded in Section 1. Employers **CANNOT** specify which document(s) they will accept from an employee.

- If an employee's name has changed at the time this form is being updated/ reverified, complete Block A.

- If an employee is rehired within three (3) years of the date this form was originally completed and the employee is still eligible to be employed on the same basis as previously indicated on this form (updating), complete Block B and the signature block.

- If an employee is rehired within three (3) years of th date this form was originally completed and th employee's work authorization has expired **or** if current employee's work authorization is about t expire (reverification), complete Block B and:
  - examine any document that reflects that th employee is authorized to work in the U.S. (se List A **or** C),
  - record the document title, document number ar expiration date (if any) in Block C, and
  - complete the signature block.

Photocopying and Retaining Form I-9. A blank I-9 may b reproduced provided both sides are copied. The Instructior must be available to all employees completing this form. Employers must retain completed I-9s for three (3) years afte the date of hire **or** one (1) year after the date employment end whichever is later.

For more detailed information, you may refer to the IN Handbook for Employers, (Form M-274). You may obtai the handbook at your local INS office.

Privacy Act Notice. The authority for collecting th information is the Immigration Reform and Control Act of 198 Pub. L. 99-603 (8 U.S.C. 1324a).

This information is for employers to verify the eligibility individuals for employment to preclude the unlawful hiring, recruiting or referring for a fee, of aliens who are not authorize to work in the United States.

This information will be used by employers as a record of the basis for determining eligibility of an employee to work in th United States. The form will be kept by the employer and mad available for inspection by officials of the U.S. Immigration an Naturalization Service, the Department of Labor, and the Offic of Special Counsel for Immigration Related Unfair Employme Practices.

Submission of the information required in this form is voluntar However, an individual may not begin employment unless th form is completed since employers are subject to civil criminal penalties if they do not comply with the Immigratio Reform and Control Act of 1986.

Reporting Burden. We try to create forms and instructions th are accurate, can be easily understood, and which impose th least possible burden on you to provide us with informatio Often this is difficult because some immigration laws are ve complex. Accordingly, the reporting burden for this collection information is computed as follows: **1)** learning about this forr 5 minutes; **2)** completing the form, 5 minutes; and **3)** assemblir and filing (recordkeeping) the form, 5 minutes, for an average 15 minutes per response. If you have comments regarding th accuracy of this burden estimate, or suggestions for making th form simpler, you can write to both the Immigration an Naturalization Service, 425 I Street, N.W., Room 530 Washington, D. C. 20536; and the Office of Management an Budget, Paperwork Reduction Project, OMB No. 1115-013 Washington, D.C. 20503.

EMPLOYERS MUST RETAIN COMPLETED I-9
PLEASE DO NOT MAIL COMPLETED I-9 TO INS

LISTS OF ACCEPTABLE DOCUMENTS

LIST A		LIST B		LIST C
Documents that Establish Both Identity and Employment Eligibility	**OR**	**Documents that Establish Identity**	**AND**	**Documents that Establish Employment Eligibility**

LIST A

Documents that Establish Both Identity and Employment Eligibility

1. U.S. Passport (unexpired or expired)

2. Certificate of U.S. Citizenship (INS Form N-560 or N-561)

3. Certificate of Naturalization (INS Form N-550 or N-570)

4. Unexpired foreign passport, with I-551 stamp or attached INS Form I-94 indicating unexpired employment authorization

5. Alien Registration Receipt Card with photograph (INS Form I-151 or I-551)

6. Unexpired Temporary Resident Card (INS Form I-688)

7. Unexpired Employment Authorization Card (INS Form I-688A)

8. Unexpired Reentry Permit (INS Form I-327)

9. Unexpired Refugee Travel Document (INS Form I-571)

10. Unexpired Employment Authorization Document issued by the INS which contains a photograph (INS Form I-688B)

OR

LIST B

Documents that Establish Identity

1. Driver's license or ID card issued by a state or outlying possession of the United States provided it contains a photograph or information such as name, date of birth, sex, height, eye color, and address

2. ID card issued by federal, state, or local government agencies or entities provided it contains a photograph or information such as name, date of birth, sex, height, eye color, and address

3. School ID card with a photograph

4. Voter's registration card

5. U.S. Military card or draft record

6. Military dependent's ID card

7. U.S. Coast Guard Merchant Mariner Card

8. Native American tribal document

9. Driver's license issued by a Canadian government authority

For persons under age 18 who are unable to present a document listed above:

10. School record or report card

11. Clinic, doctor, or hospital record

12. Day-care or nursery school record

AND

LIST C

Documents that Establish Employment Eligibility

1. U.S. social security card issued by the Social Security Administration (other than a card stating it is not valid for employment)

2. Certification of Birth Abroad issued by the Department of State (Form FS-545 or Form DS-1350)

3. Original or certified copy of a birth certificate issued by a state, county, municipal authority or outlying possession of the United States bearing an official seal

4. Native American tribal document

5. U.S. Citizen ID Card (INS Form I-197)

6. ID Card for use of Resident Citizen in the United States (INS Form I-179)

7. Unexpired employment authorization document issued by the INS (other than those listed under List A)

Illustrations of many of these documents appear In Part 8 of the Handbook for Employers (M-274)

Form I-9 (Rev. 11-21-91) N

PARTNERSHIP AGREEMENT

This Partnership Agreement is entered into this _____ day of _____,
_____, by and between the following partners: _____
_____,
who agree as follows:

1. **Name of Partnership.** The name of the partnership shall be: _____
    _____.
    The name under which the partnership shall conduct business shall be: _____
    _____.

2. **Principal Place of Business.** The partnership's principal place of business shall be:
    _____.

3. **Purpose of Partnership.** The purposes of the partnership are: _____
    _____.
    In addition to the specific purposes set forth above, the purpose of the partnership is
    also to conduct any lawful business in which the partners, from time to time, may agree
    to become engaged.

4. **Term of Partnership.** The partnership shall become effective as of the date of this agree-
    ment, and shall continue until it is dissolved by all of the partners, or until a partner
    leaves for any reason including incapacity or death, or until otherwise dissolved by law.

5. **Contributions of Partners.** Each partner shall make an initial cash contribution to the
    partnership in the amount of $_____.

6. **Profits and Losses / Ownership Interests.** The partners shall share equally in the prof-
    its and losses of the partnership.

7. **Voting Rights.** All partnership decisions must be made by the unanimous agreement of
    the partners. All matters not referred to in this agreement shall be determined accord-
    ing to this paragraph.

8. **Transfer of a Partnership Interest.**

    A. **Option of Partnership to Purchase / Right of First Refusal.** In the event any part-
        ner leaves the partnership; for whatever reason including voluntary withdrawal or
        retirement, incapacity, or death; the remaining partners shall have the option to pur-
        chase said partner's interest from said partner or his or her estate. In the event any
        partner receives, and is willing to accept, an offer from a person who is not a part-
        ner to purchase all of his or her interest in the partnership, he or she shall notify the
        other partners of the identity of the proposed buyer, the amount and terms of the
        offer, and of his or her willingness to accept the offer. The other partners shall then

have the option, within 30 days after notice is given, to purchase that partner's interest in the partnership name on the same terms as those of the offer of the person who is not a partner, or to put the business up for sale, or to dissolve the partnership.

B. **Valuation of Partnership.** In the event the remaining partners exercise the right to purchase the other's interest as provided above, the value of the partnership shall be net worth of the partnership as of the date of such purchase. Net worth shall be determined by the market value of the following assets: all of the partnership's real and personal property, liquid assets, accounts receivable, earned but unbilled fees, and money earned for work in progress; less the total amount of all debts owed by the partnership.

C. **Payment Upon Buy-Out.** In the event the remaining partners exercise the right to purchase the other's interest as provided above, the remaining partners shall pay the departing partner for his or her interest by way of a promissory note of the partnership, dated as of the date of purchase, which shall mature in not more than _____ years, and shall bear interest at the rate of _____% per annum. The first payment shall be made _____ days after the date of the promissory note.

9. **Governing Law.** This agreement shall be governed by the laws of _____.

10. **Severability.** If any part of this agreement is adjudged invalid, illegal, or unenforceable, the remaining parts shall not be affected and shall remain in full force and effect.

11. **Binding Agreement / No Other Beneficiary.** This agreement shall be binding upon the parties, and upon their heirs, executors, personal representatives, administrators, and assigns. No person shall have a right or cause of action arising or resulting from this agreement except those who are parties to it and their successors in interest.

12. **Entire Agreement.** This instrument, including any attached exhibits, constitutes the entire agreement of the parties. No representations or promises have been made except those that are set out in this agreement. This agreement may not be modified except in writing signed by the parties.

13. **Paragraph Headings.** The headings of the paragraphs contained in this agreement are for convenience only, and are not to be considered a part of this agreement or used in determining its content or context.

_____   _____
Signature   Signature

_____   _____
Signature   Signature

_____   _____
Signature   Signature

LIMITED POWER OF ATTORNEY

_____ (the "Grantor") hereby grants to _____ (the "Agent") a limited power of attorney. As the Grantor's attorney in fact, the Agent shall have full power and authority to undertake and perform the following on behalf of the Grantor:

By accepting this grant, the Agent agrees to act in a fiduciary capacity consistent with the reasonable best interests of the Grantor. This power of attorney may be revoked by the Grantor at any time; however, any person dealing with the Agent as attorney in fact may rely on this appointment until receipt of actual notice of termination.

IN WITNESS WHEREOF, the undersigned grantor has executed this power of attorney under seal as of the date stated above.

Attest:_____   _____(Seal)

,Secretary   , Grantor

STATE OF
COUNTY OF

I certify that _____ ,who ❑ is personally known to me to be the person whose name is subscribed to the foregoing instrument   ❑ produced _____ as identification, personally appeared before me on _____, and ❑ acknowledged the execution of the foregoing instrument ❑ acknowledged that (s)he is (Assistant) Secretary of _____ _____and that by authority duly given and as the act of the corporation, the foregoing instrument was signed in its name by its (Vice) President, sealed with its corporate seal and attested by him/her as its (Assistant) Secretary.

_____

Notary Public, State of

Notary's commission expires:

I hereby accept the foregoing appointment as attorney in fact on _____.

_____

Attorney in Fact

POWER OF ATTORNEY

_____ (the "Grantor")
hereby grants to _____(the "Agent")
a general power of attorney. As the Grantor's attorney in fact, the Agent shall have full power and authority to undertake any and all acts which may be lawfully undertaken on behalf of the grantor including but not limited to the right to buy, sell, lease, mortgage, assign, rent or otherwise dispose of any real or personal property belonging to the Grantor; to execute, accept, undertake and perform contracts in the name of the Grantor; to deposit, endorse, or withdraw funds to or from any bank depository of the Grantor; to initiate, defend or settle legal actions on behalf of the Grantor; and to retain any accountant, attorney or other advisor deemed by the Agent to be necessary to protect the interests of the Grantor in relation to such powers.

By accepting this grant, the Agent agrees to act in a fiduciary capacity consistent with the reasonable best interests of the Grantor. This power of attorney may be revoked by the Grantor at any time; however, any person dealing with the Agent as attorney in fact may rely on this appointment until receipt of actual notice of termination.

IN WITNESS WHEREOF, the undersigned grantor has executed this power of attorney under seal as of the date stated above.

Attest:_____   _____(Seal)
                      ,Secretary   , Grantor

STATE OF
COUNTY OF

I certify that _____ ,who ❑ is personally known to me to be the person whose name is subscribed to the foregoing instrument   ❑ produced _____ as identification, personally appeared before me on _____, and ❑ acknowledged the execution of the foregoing instrument ❑ acknowledged that (s)he is (Assistant) Secretary of _____ _____and that by authority duly given and as the act of the corporation, the foregoing instrument was signed in its name by its (Vice) President, sealed with its corporate seal and attested by him/her as its (Assistant) Secretary.

_____

Notary Public, State of

Notary's commission expires:

I hereby accept the foregoing appointment as attorney in fact on _____.

_____

Attorney in Fact

BILL OF SALE

For valuable consideration, the receipt and sufficiency of which is hereby acknowledged, the undersigned hereby sells and transfers to _____ the following:

The undersigned warrants and represents that it has good title to and full authority to sell and transfer the same and that the property is sold and transferred free and clear of all liens, claims and encumbrances except:

Executed under seal on _____.

_____

BILL OF SALE

For valuable consideration, the receipt and sufficiency of which is hereby acknowledged, the undersigned hereby sells and transfers to _____ the following:

The undersigned warrants and represents that it has good title to and full authority to sell and transfer the same and that the property is sold and transferred free and clear of all liens, claims and encumbrances except:

The undersigned warrants that, subject to the exceptions stated above, it will indemnify the Buyer, and defend title to the property, against the adverse claims of all persons.

Executed under seal on _____.

_____

CREDIT APPLICATION

❑ Individual

❑ Business: ❑ Corporation   ❑ Partnership   ❑ Other: _____

Annual gross sales $_____   Annual net profit $_____   Net value $_____

Name:	Address:
Social Security Number:	
Spouse's Name:	
Spouse's Social Security Number:	Telephone:

Previous Address(es):

Employer (name, address & phone)	Previous Employer:
Position:	Position:
Annual Income:	Annual Income:
Spouse's Employer (name, address & phone)	Spouse's Previous Employer:
Position:	Position:
Annual Income:	Annual Income:

Other Income:

Bank & Credit References:

Trade References:

If a business, state names & addresses of owners, partners, or officers:

NOTE

$_____   Date:_____

_____ hereby
promises to pay to the order of _____
_____ the sum of $_____,
with interest thereon from the date of this note to the date of payment at the rate of interest per annum as set forth below:

    This note is due a payable in full on _____, if not paid sooner.
The principal and interest shall be payable when due at _____
_____ or at a place
of which the undersigned may be notified in writing by the holder of this note.

    This note is not assumable without the written consent of the lender. This note may be paid in whole or in part at any time prior without penalty. The borrower waives demand, presentment, protest, and notice. This note shall be fully payable upon demand of any holder in the event the undersigned shall default on the terms of this note or any agreement securing the payment of this note. In the event of default, the undersigned agrees to pay all costs of collection including reasonable attorneys fees.

    IN WITNESS WHEREOF, the undersigned has executed this note under seal as of the date stated above (if the undersigned is a corporation, this note has been executed under seal and by authority of its board of directors).

                                        _____

                                        _____

ASSIGNMENT OF MORTGAGE

For and in consideration of _____,
the receipt of which is hereby acknowledged, _____
_____ hereby assigns, grants, and transfers to
_____,
_____ that certain mortgage dated _____,
executed by _____,
and recorded at _____
_____, together
with the note described therein and the money together with the interest due thereon.

IN WITNESS WHEREOF, the undersigned has executed this assignment on the
_____ day of _____, _____.

Witnessed by: _____

_____

_____

STATE OF   )
COUNTY OF   )

I certify that _____ ,who ❑ is personally known
to me to be the person whose name is subscribed to the foregoing instrument   ❑ produced
_____ as identification, personally appeared before me
on _____, and ❑ acknowledged the execution of the foregoing
instrument ❑ acknowledged that (s)he is (Assistant) Secretary of _____
_____and that by authority duly given and
as the act of the corporation, the foregoing instrument was signed in its name by its (Vice)
President, sealed with its corporate seal and attested by him/her as its (Assistant) Secretary.

_____

Notary Public, State of

My commission expires:

SATISFACTION OF MORTGAGE

For value received, _____,
the holder(s) of that certain mortgage dated _____, executed by
_____,
and recorded at _____
_____,
hereby acknowledge(s) full payment, satisfaction and discharge of said mortgage.

IN WITNESS WHEREOF, the undersigned has executed this satisfaction of mortgage
on the _____ day of _____, _____.

Witnesses by: _____

_____

_____

STATE OF   )
COUNTY OF   )

I certify that _____ ,who ❏ is personally known
to me to be the person whose name is subscribed to the foregoing instrument ❏ produced
_____ as identification, personally appeared before me
on _____, and ❏ acknowledged the execution of the foregoing
instrument ❏ acknowledged that (s)he is (Assistant) Secretary of _____
_____and that by authority duly given and
as the act of the corporation, the foregoing instrument was signed in its name by its (Vice)
President, sealed with its corporate seal and attested by him/her as its (Assistant) Secretary.

_____
Notary Public, State of

My commission expires:

AMENDMENT TO LEASE AGREEMENT

For valuable consideration, the receipt and sufficiency of which is hereby acknowledged by each of the parties, this agreement amends a lease agreement (the "Lease") between _____ (the "Landlord") and _____ (the "Tenant") dated_____, relating to property located at _____ _____.

This agreement is hereby incorporated into the Lease.

Except as changed by this amendment, the Lease shall continue in effect according to its terms. The amendments herein shall be effective on the date this document is executed by both parties.

Executed on _____.

Landlord: Tenant:

_____   _____

_____   _____

LEASE ASSIGNMENT

This Lease Assignment is entered into by and among _____ (the "Assignor"), _____ (the "Assignee"), and _____ (the "Landlord"). For valuable consideration, it is agreed by the parties as follows:

1. The Landlord and the Assignor have entered into a lease agreement (the "Lease") dated _____, concerning the premises described as:

2. The Assignor hereby assigns and transfers to the Assignee all of Assignor's rights and delegates all of Assignor's duties under the Lease effective _____ (the "Effective Date").

3. The Assignee hereby accepts such assignment of rights and delegation of duties and agrees to pay all rents promptly when due and perform all of Assignor's obligations under the Lease accruing on and after the Effective Date. The Assignee further agrees to indemnify and hold the Assignor harmless from any breach of Assignee's duties hereunder.

4. ❏ The Assignor agrees to transfer possession of the leased premises to the Assignee on the Effective Date. All rents and obligations of the Assignor under the Lease accruing before the Effective Date shall have been paid or discharged.

❏ The Landlord hereby assents to the assignment of the Lease hereunder and as of the Effective Date hereby releases and discharges the Assignor from all duties and obligations under the Lease accruing after the Effective Date.

❏ The Landlord hereby assents to this lease assignment provided that the Landlord's assent shall not discharge the Assignor of any obligations under the Lease in the event of breach by the Assignee. The Landlord will give notice to the Assignor of any breach by the Assignee. If the Assignor pays all accrued rents and cures any other default of the Assignee, the Assignor may enforce the terms of the Lease and this Assignment against the Assignee, in the name of the Landlord, if necessary.

5. There shall be no further assignment of the Lease without the written consent of the Landlord.

6. This agreement shall be binding upon and inure to the benefit of the parties, their successors, assigns and personal representatives.

This assignment was executed under seal on _____.

Assignor: Assignee:

_____   _____

_____   _____

Landlord:

_____

_____

Landlord's Consent to Sublease

FOR VALUABLE CONSIDERATION, the undersigned (the "Landlord") hereby consents to the sublease of all or part of the premises located at _____ _____ which is the subject of a lease agreement between Landlord and _____ (the "Tenant"), pursuant to an Agreement to Sublease dated _____, between the Tenant and _____ as Subtenant dated _____.

This consent was signed by the Landlord on _____.

Landlord:

_____

Security Agreement

In exchange for valuable consideration, the receipt and sufficiency of which is hereby acknowledged by the undersigned, _____
(the "Debtor") hereby grants to _____
(the "Creditor") a security interest in _____
to secure the payment and performance of the Debtor's obligations described as follows (the "Obligations"):

Upon any default by the Debtor in the performance of any of the Obligations, the Creditor may declare all obligations of the Debtor immediately due and payable and shall have the remedies of a secured party under the Uniform Commercial Code enacted in the state the laws of which govern the terms of this agreement.

This agreement is executed by the Debtor under seal on _____.

_____

_____

DISCHARGE OF SECURITY INTEREST

The undersigned, _____
(the "Creditor") hereby discharges and releases _____
_____ (the "Debtor") from the Security
Agreement dated _____, _____, covering the following property:

Any claims or obligations that are not specifically stated in this instrument are not released or discharged by this instrument. No assignment of any claim or obligation stated in this instrument has been made by the Creditor. The Creditor agrees to execute a Release of UCC Financing Statement, if requested by the Debtor.

This agreement is executed by the Creditor under seal on _____.

_____

_____

NOTICE OF REJECTION OF NON-CONFORMING GOODS

Date:_____

TO:

RE: Purchase Order No._____

We hereby reject the delivery of the goods specified in the above-mentioned purchase order. We received delivery on _____, _____, however, the goods do not conform to the specifications and requirements of our purchase order for the following reasons:

We paid for the goods with check number _____, dated _____, in the sum of $_____. In the event you have not yet cashed this check, please return the check to us. If the check has been cashed, we hereby demand a refund of this amount. If we do not receive a refund within _____ days of the date of this Notice, we will take legal action for the refund.

Please notify us of your desires regarding the of the goods at your expense. If we do not receive instructions within _____ days of the date of this Notice, we will not accept any responsibility for storage.

Please be advised that we reserve all rights available to us under the Uniform Commercial Code and any other applicable law.

_____

NOTICE OF CONDITIONAL ACCEPTANCE OF NON-CONFORMING GOODS

Date:_____

TO:

RE: Purchase Order No._____

    You are hereby notified that the goods delivered to us on _____, pursuant to the above-mentioned purchase order, do not conform to the specifications and requirements of our purchase order for the following reasons:

    Although we are under no obligation to accept such non-conforming goods, we are willing to accept them on the following condition(s):

    If you do not notify us in writing that you are accepting these terms within _____ days of the date of this Notice, we will reject the goods and they will be returned to you at your expense.

    Please be advised that we reserve all rights available to us under the Uniform Commercial Code and any other applicable law.

_____

DEMAND FOR PAYMENT

Date:_____

TO:

Your account is delinquent in the amount of $_____.

Please be advised that in the event we do not receive payment in full within _____ days of the date of this notice, we will initiate collection proceedings against you without further notice. If such proceedings are initiated, you will also be responsible for pre-judgment interest, attorneys' fees, court costs, and any and all other costs of collection. Collection proceedings may also adversely affect your credit rating.

If full payment has already been sent, please disregard this notice.

Please contact the undersigned if you have any questions.

_____

Notice of Assignment of Account for Collection

Date:_____

TO:

    Please be advised that your delinquent account has been assigned for collection to the following collection agent: _____
_____.

The amount assigned is based upon the following amount(s):

    Please contact the above-mentioned collection agent regarding this notice and all future payments on this account.

_____

CONTRACT FOR SERVICES

This agreement is made between _____
(the "Company") and _____
(the "Customer"). The Company and the Customer agree as follows:

1. The Company will provide the following services to the Customer under the terms and conditions of this agreement:

2. The Company agrees to perform such services diligently using its best efforts and providing competent personnel and adequate time to complete the work to professional standards of high quality. The Company may perform such services at the times and locations as may be agreed by the parties.

3. As payment for the completed services described above, and in addition to the release provided in paragraph 5 below, the Customer shall pay to the Company the sum of $_____ payable in the following manner:

4. The services to be provided by the Company pursuant to this agreement shall begin not later than _____, and shall be completed not later than _____.

5. DISCLAIMER OF LIABILITY AND RELEASE BY CUSTOMER-READ CAREFULLY: The Company has informed the Customer, and the Customer acknowledges having been informed that the performance of the services described above involves certain inherent risks and dangers including, but not limited to the following:

THE COMPANY DISCLAIMS ALL LIABILITY FOR DAMAGES AND INJURIES THAT MAY RESULT FROM ALL RISKS REFERRED TO IN THIS PARAGRAPH, and the Customer, having been so informed, in further consideration of the Company's willingness to provide such services, hereby releases, discharges and acquits the Company, and its employees, agents, successors and assigns, from any and all claims, actions, suits, or liabilities that may arise as a result of or in connection with the performance of the services not resulting directly and wholly from the negligence of the Company, its agents and employees.

6. The parties agree that no employer - employee relationship is created by this agreement, but that the relationship of the Company to the Customer shall be that of an independent contractor.

7. This agreement shall be governed by the laws of _____.

8. If any part of this agreement is adjudged invalid, illegal, or unenforceable, the remaining parts shall not be affected and shall remain in full force and effect.

9. This agreement shall be binding upon the parties, and upon their heirs, executors, personal representatives, administrators, and assigns. No person shall have a right or cause of action arising out of or resulting from this agreement except those who are parties to it and their successors in interest.

10. This instrument, including any attached exhibits and addenda, constitutes the entire agreement of the parties. No representations or promises have been made except those that are set out in this agreement. This agreement may not be modified except in writing signed by all the parties.

IN WITNESS WHEREOF the parties have signed this agreement under seal on _____.

_____   _____

_____   _____

MEDIATION AGREEMENT

The undersigned parties are engaged in a dispute regarding _____.
We hereby agree to submit such dispute to mediation by _____ and that all matters resolved in mediation shall be reduced to a binding written agreement signed by the parties. The costs of mediation shall be borne equally by the parties.

Dated:_____.

_____   _____

_____   _____

ARBITRATION AGREEMENT

This Arbitration Agreement is made this _____ day of _____, _____, by and between _____ and _____, who agree as follows:

1. The parties agree that any controversy, claim or dispute arising out of or related to:

shall be submitted to arbitration. Such arbitration shall take place at _____ or at such other place as may be agreed upon by the parties.

2. The parties shall attempt to agree on one arbitrator. If they are unable to so agree, then each party shall appoint one arbitrator and those appointed shall appoint a third arbitrator.

3. The expenses of arbitration shall be divided equally by the parties.

4. The arbitrators shall conclusively decide all issues of law and fact related to the arbitrated dispute. Judgment upon an award rendered by the arbitrator may be entered in any court having jurisdiction.

5. The prevailing party ❏ shall ❏ shall not be entitled to reasonable attorneys' fees.

_____   _____

_____   _____

WAIVER AND ASSUMPTION OF RISK

I, _____,
hereby voluntarily sign this Waiver and Assumption of Risk in favor of
_____ (the "Company"),
fully waiving and releasing the Company from any and all claims for personal injury, property damage, or death that may result from my use of the Company's facilities or property, or from my participation in the following activities or instruction ("activities"):

I sign this Waiver and Assumption of Risk in consideration of the opportunity to use the Company's facilities or property, receive instruction from the Company and its employees, or to participate in Company-sponsored activities as described above.

I acknowledge and understand that there are dangers and risks associated with the activities described above, which have been fully explained to me. I fully assume the dangers and risks, and agree to use my best judgment in engaging in those activities and to follow the safety instructions provided.

I am a competent adult, aged _____, and I freely and voluntarily assume the risks associated with the activities described above.

Dated:_____

Witness:_____

Name:_____
Address:_____
_____
Telephone:_____

In case of emergency, please contact:

Name:_____
Address:_____
_____
Telephone:_____
Relationship:_____

GENERAL RELEASE

In exchange for the sum of $10.00 and other valuable consideration, the receipt and sufficiency of which is hereby acknowledged, the undersigned corporation hereby forever releases, discharges and acquits _____,
and [its/his/her] successors, assigns, heirs and personal representatives, from any and all claims, actions, suits, agreements or liabilities in favor of or owed to the undersigned, existing at any time up to the date of this release.

IN WITNESS WHEREOF, the undersigned has executed this release under seal on _____.

_____

SPECIFIC RELEASE

In exchange for the sum of $10.00 and other valuable consideration, the receipt and sufficiency of which is hereby acknowledged, the undersigned hereby forever releases, discharges and acquits _____,
and [its/his/her] successors, assigns, heirs and personal representatives, from any and all claims, actions, suits, agreements or liabilities arising out of or related to:

IN WITNESS WHEREOF, the undersigned has executed this release under seal on
_____.

_____

MUTUAL RELEASE

In exchange for the sum of $10.00 and other valuable consideration, the receipt and sufficiency of which is hereby acknowledged, the undersigned hereby forever release, discharge and acquit each other, and their successors, assigns, heirs and personal representatives, from any and all claims, actions, suits, agreements or liabilities arising out of or related to:

IN WITNESS WHEREOF, the undersigned have executed this release under seal on

_____.

_____   _____

_____   _____

Covenant Not to Sue

This agreement is made by and between _____
_____ (the "Covenantor"), for [itself/himself/herself]
and for its heirs, legal representatives and assigns, and _____
_____ (the "Covenantee").

    1. In exchange for the Covenantor's covenant herein, the Covenantee
_____
_____
_____
_____.

    2. In exchange for the consideration stated in paragraph 1 above, the receipt and sufficiency of which is hereby acknowledged by the Covenantor, the Covenantor covenants with the Covenantee never to institute any suit or action at law or in equity against the Covenantee by reason of any claim the Covenantor now has or may hereafter acquire related to: _____
_____.

    This agreement was executed by the parties under seal on _____.

Covenantor: Covenantee:

_____   _____

_____   _____

RELEASE OF JUDGMENT

The Plaintiff, _____, hereby acknowledges that the judgment in this action has been fully satisfied by the Defendant, _____, and hereby releases and discharges said Defendant from any and all further liability for said judgment.

Dated:_____.

_____

Release of Liens

The undersigned [sub]contractor has furnished construction materials and/or labor in connection with repairs or construction at the property described as (insert legal property description, street address, recording information, or other appropriate information:

(hereinafter called the "Premises"). The undersigned hereby releases all liens and rights to file liens against the Premises for any and all such materials or services provided through the date of this release.

The date of this release is _____.

Contractor/Subcontractor:

_____

_____

AFFIDAVIT

The undersigned, being first duly sworn, deposes and says:

This affidavit was executed by me on _____.

_____

STATE OF   )
COUNTY OF   )

    I certify that _____ ,who ❏ is personally known to me to be the person whose name is subscribed to the foregoing instrument ❏ produced _____ as identification, personally appeared before me on _____, and ❏ acknowledged the execution of the foregoing instrument ❏ acknowledged that (s)he is (Assistant) Secretary of _____ _____and that by authority duly given and as the act of the corporation, the foregoing instrument was signed in its name by its (Vice) President, sealed with its corporate seal and attested by him/her as its (Assistant) Secretary.

_____

Notary Public, State of

My commission expires:

CASH RECEIPT

The undersigned hereby certifies and acknowledges that on _____,
(s)he received from _____
❑ the cash sum of $_____   ❑ a check in the amount of $_____
in payment for:

_____

RECEIPT FOR PERSONAL PROPERTY

The undersigned hereby certifies and acknowledges that on _____,
(s)he received from _____
the following personal property:

The purpose for which such items were received was:

_____

SALES AGREEMENT

This agreement is made by and between _____ _____ (the "Seller") and _____ _____, (the Buyer), who agree as follows:

1. The Seller agrees to sell, and the Buyer agrees to buy:

2. In exchange for the Property, the Buyer agrees to pay to the Seller the sum of $_____, payable according to the terms of a promissory note a copy of which is attached to this agreement and incorporated into this agreement by reference (the "Note").

3. The Seller retains a security interest in the Property to secure payment and performance of the Buyer's obligations under this agreement and the Note. Upon any default by the Buyer in the performance of any such obligations, the Seller may declare all obligations immediately due and payable and shall have the remedies of a secured party under the Uniform Commercial Code enacted in the state the laws of which govern the terms of this agreement.

4. This agreement shall be governed by the laws of _____.

5. If any part of this agreement is adjudged invalid, illegal, or unenforceable, the remaining parts shall not be affected and shall remain in full force and effect.

6. This agreement shall be binding upon the parties, and upon their heirs, executors, personal representatives, administrators, and assigns. No person shall have a right or cause of action arising out of or resulting from this agreement except those who are parties to it and their successors in interest.

7. This instrument, including any attached exhibits and addenda, constitutes the entire agreement of the parties. No representations or promises have been made except those that are set out in this agreement. This agreement may not be modified except in writing signed by all the parties.

IN WITNESS WHEREOF the parties have signed this agreement under seal on _____.

Seller: Buyer:

_____   _____

_____   _____

CONSIGNMENT SALE AGREEMENT

This agreement is made by and between _____ (the "Consignor") and _____ (the "Consignee").

1. The Consignor and Consignee acknowledge and agree that the Consignor has provided the goods described below to Consignee for sale on a consignment basis, for the prices indicated, under the terms and conditions of this agreement:

2. The Consignee agrees to use its best efforts to sell the goods, for cash, for the benefit of the Consignor and to account to the Consignor for such sales within _____, delivering the sale proceeds to the Consignor, less commission, at the time of the accounting.

3. The Consignee agrees to accept as its commission, in full payment for its performance under this agreement, an amount equal to _____% of the gross sales price of the goods exclusive of any sales taxes.

4. Any goods the Consignee is unable to sell may be returned to the Consignor at the expense of the Consignee. The Consignor may reclaim unsold goods at any time.

5. At the request of the Consignor, the Consignee agrees to execute financing statements perfecting the Consignor's claim of ownership of the goods.

6. This agreement shall be governed by the laws of _____.

7. If any part of this agreement is adjudged invalid, illegal, or unenforceable, the remaining parts shall not be affected and shall remain in full force and effect.

8. This agreement shall be binding upon the parties, and upon their heirs, executors, personal representatives, administrators, and assigns. No person shall have a right or cause of action arising out of or resulting from this agreement except those who are parties to it and their successors in interest.

9. This instrument, including any attached exhibits and addenda, constitutes the entire agreement of the parties. No representations or promises have been made except those that are set out in this agreement. This agreement may not be modified except in writing signed by all the parties.

IN WITNESS WHEREOF the parties have signed this agreement under seal on _____.

Consignor: Consignee:

_____   _____

_____   _____

PERSONAL PROPERTY LEASE AGREEMENT

This agreement is made by and between _____ _____(the "Lessor") and _____ _____ (the "Lessee").

1. The Lessor hereby leases to the Lessee, and the Lessee hereby leases from the lessor, beginning on _____ and terminating on _____, the property described below (the "Property"):

2. The Lessee shall pay to the Lessor as rent the sum of $_____ per month payable in advance on or before the _____ day of each month, the first such payment being due on _____. Payment of rent shall be made to the Lessor at the following address: _____.

3. The Lessee agrees to use the Property in a careful manner and in compliance with applicable laws and regulations and, at the end of the lease term shall return the Property to the Lessor in the same condition as it was received by the Lessee, normal wear and tear excepted.

4. The Lessor shall not be liable for any liability, loss, or damage caused by the Property or its use that does not result directly and wholly from the negligence of the Lessor.

5. This agreement shall be governed by the laws of _____.

6. If any part of this agreement is adjudged invalid, illegal, or unenforceable, the remaining parts shall not be affected and shall remain in full force and effect.

7. This agreement shall be binding upon the parties, and upon their heirs, executors, personal representatives, administrators, and assigns. No person shall have a right or cause of action arising out of or resulting from this agreement except those who are parties to it and their successors in interest.

8. This instrument, including any attached exhibits and addenda, constitutes the entire agreement of the parties. No representations or promises have been made except those that are set out in this agreement. This agreement may not be modified except in writing signed by all the parties.

IN WITNESS WHEREOF the parties have signed this agreement under seal on _____.

Lessor: Lessee:

_____   _____

_____   _____

INDEX

Your #1 Source for Real World Legal Information...

LEGAL SURVIVAL GUIDES™

- Written by lawyers
- Simple English explanation of the law
- Forms and instructions included

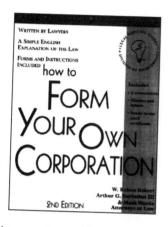

HOW TO FORM YOUR OWN CORPORATION (2ND EDITION)

This simple guide contains a summary of the laws and forms with instructions for forming a corporation in all 50 states and the District of Columbia. New business owners can save precious capital by forming their own corporation.

208 pages; $19.95;
ISBN 1-57071-227-1

THE MOST VALUABLE CORPORATE FORMS YOU'LL EVER NEED (2ND EDITION)

Running a corporation requires many forms, and smaller organizations cannot always afford to have an attorney on retainer for every occasion. This book provides over 100 forms for all types of corporate situations.

224 pages; $24.95;
ISBN 1-57071-346-4

THE MOST VALUABLE PERSONAL LEGAL FORMS YOU'LL EVER NEED

Many basic legal situations require only a simple legal form. This book contains the most commonly needed forms. Why pay a lawyer hundreds of dollars for simple forms when you can fill them out yourself?

144 pages; $14.95;
ISBN 1-57071-347-2

What our customers say about our books:

"It couldn't be more clear for the lay person." —R.D.

"I want you to know I really appreciate your book. It has saved me a lot of time and money." —L.T.

"Your real estate contracts book has saved me nearly $12,000.00 in closing costs over the past year." —A.B.

"...many of the legal questions that I have had over the years were answered clearly and concisely through your plain English interpretation of the law." —C.E.H.

"If there weren't people out there like you I'd be lost. You have the best books of this type out there." —S.B.

"...your forms and directions are easy to follow." —C.V.M.

Legal Survival Guides are directly available from the publisher, or from your local bookstores.
For credit card orders call 1–800–43–BRIGHT, write P.O. Box 372, Naperville, IL 60566,
or fax 630-961-2168

LEGAL SURVIVAL GUIDES™ NATIONAL TITLES
Valid in All 50 States

LEGAL SURVIVAL IN BUSINESS

How to Form Your Own Corporation (2E)	$19.95
How to Register Your Own Copyright (2E)	$19.95
How to Register Your Own Trademark (2E)	$19.95
Most Valuable Business Forms You'll Ever Need	$19.95
Most Valuable Corporate Forms You'll Ever Need	$24.95
Software Law (with diskette)	$29.95

LEGAL SURVIVAL IN COURT

Crime Victim's Guide to Justice	$19.95
Debtors' Rights (2E)	$12.95
Defend Yourself Against Criminal Charges	$19.95
Grandparents' Rights	$19.95
Help Your Lawyer Win Your Case	$12.95
Jurors' Rights	$9.95
Legal Malpractice and Other Claims Against Your Lawyer	$18.95
Legal Research Made Easy	$14.95
Simple Ways to Protect Yourself From Lawsuits	$24.95
Victim's Rights	$12.95
Winning Your Personal Injury Claim	$19.95

LEGAL SURVIVAL IN REAL ESTATE

How to Buy a Condominium or Townhome	$16.95
How to Negotiate Real Estate Contracts (3E)	$16.95
How to Negotiate Real Estate Leases (3E)	$16.95
Successful Real Estate Brokerage Management	$19.95

LEGAL SURVIVAL IN PERSONAL AFFAIRS

How to File Your Own Bankruptcy (4E)	$19.95
How to File Your Own Divorce (3E)	$19.95
How to Make Your Own Will	$12.95
How to Write Your Own Living Will	$9.95
How to Win Your Unemployment Compensation	$19.95
Living Trusts and Simple Ways to Avoid Probate	$19.95
Neighbor vs. Neighbor	$12.95
Power of Attorney Handbook (2E)	$19.95
Social Security Benefits Handbook	$14.95
U.S.A. Immigration Guide (2E)	$19.95
Guia de Inmigracion a Estados Unidos	$19.95

Legal Survival Guides are directly available from the publisher, or from your local bookstores.

For credit card orders call 1–800–43–BRIGHT, write P.O. Box 372, Naperville, IL 60566, or fax 630-961-2168

LEGAL SURVIVAL GUIDES™ STATE TITLES
Up-to-date for Your State

CALIFORNIA

How to File for Divorce in CA	$19.95
How to Make a CA Will	$12.95
How to Start a Business in CA	$16.95
How to Win in Small Claims Court in CA	$14.95
Landlords' Rights and Duties in CA	$19.95
CA Power of Attorney Handbook	$19.95

FLORIDA

Florida Power of Attorney Handbook	$9.95
How to Change Your Name in FL (3E)	$14.95
How to File a FL Construction Lien (2E)	$19.95
How to File a Guardianship in FL	$19.95
How to File for Divorce in FL (4E)	$21.95
How to Form a Nonprofit Corp in FL (3E)	$19.95
How to Form a Simple Corp in FL (3E)	$19.95
How to Make a FL Will (5E)	$12.95
How to Modify Your FL Divorce Judgement (3E)	$22.95
How to Probate an Estate in FL (2E)	$24.95
How to Start a Business in FL (4E)	$16.95
How to Win in Small Claims Court in FL (6E)	$14.95
Land Trusts in FL (5E)	$24.95
Landlords' Rights and Duties in FL (7E)	$19.95
Women's Legal Rights in FL	$19.95

GEORGIA

How to File for Divorce in GA (2E)	$19.95
How to Make a GA Will (2E)	$9.95
How to Start and Run a GA Business (2E)	$18.95

ILLINOIS

How to File for Divorce in IL	$19.95
How to Make an IL Will	$9.95
How to Start a Business in IL	$16.95

MASSACHUSETTS

How to File for Divorce in MA (2E)	$19.95
How to Make a MA Will	$9.95
How to Probate an Estate in MA	$19.95
How to Start a Business in MA	$16.95
Landlords' Rights and Duties in MA	$19.95

MICHIGAN

How to File for Divorce in MI	$19.95
How to Make a MI Will	$9.95
How to Start a Business in MI	$16.95

MINNESOTA

How to File for Divorce in MN	$19.95
How to Form a Simple Corporation in MN	$19.95
How to Make a MN Will	$9.95
How to Start a Business in MN	$16.95

NEW YORK

How to File for Divorce in NY	$19.95
How to Make a NY Will	$12.95
How to Start a Business in NY	$16.95
How to Win in Small Claims Court in NY	$14.95
Landlords' Rights and Duties in NY	$19.95
New York Power of Attorney Handbook	$12.95

NORTH CAROLINA

How to File for Divorce in NC (2E)	$19.95
How to Make a NC Will (2E)	$9.95
How to Start a Business in NC	$16.95

PENNSYLVANIA

How to File for Divorce in PA	$19.95
How to Make a PA Will	$12.95
How to Start a Business in PA	$16.95
Landlords' Rights and Duties in PA	$19.95

TEXAS

How to File for Divorce in TX (2E)	$19.95
How to Form a Simple Corporation in TX	$19.95
How to Make a TX Will	$9.95
How to Probate an Estate in TX	$19.95
How to Start a Business in TX	$16.95
How to Win in Small Claims Court in TX	$14.95
Landlords' Rights and Duties in TX	$19.95

Legal Survival Guides are directly available from the publisher, or from your local bookstores.
For credit card orders call 1–800–43–BRIGHT, write P.O. Box 372, Naperville, IL 60566,
or fax 630-961-2168

LEGAL SURVIVAL GUIDES™ ORDER FORM

BILL TO:		SHIP TO:	
Phone #	Terms	F.O.B. Chicago, IL	Ship Date

Charge my: ☐ VISA   ☐ MasterCard   ☐ American Express

☐ Money Order or Personal Check

Credit Card Number [ ][ ][ ][ ][ ][ ][ ][ ][ ][ ][ ][ ][ ][ ]

Expiration Date [ ][ ][ ][ ]

Qty	ISBN	Title	Retail	Ext.
		LEGAL SURVIVAL GUIDES SPRING 1998 NATIONAL FRONTLIST		
___	1-57071-342-1	Debtors' Rights (3E)	$12.95	___
___	1-57071-343-X	How to Form Your Own Partnership	$19.95	___
___	1-57071-331-6	How to Negotiate Real Estate Contracts (3E)	$16.95	___
___	1-57071-332-4	How to Negotiate Real Estate Leases (3E)	$16.95	___
___	1-57071-349-9	How to Win Your Unemployment Compensation Claim	$19.95	___
___	1-57071-344-8	How to Write Your Own Premarital Agreement (2E)	$19.95	___
___	1-57071-333-2	Jurors' Rights (2E)	$9.95	___
___	1-57071-336-7	Living Trusts and Simple Ways to Avoid Probate (2E)	$19.95	___
___	1-57071-345-6	Most Valuable Bus. Legal Forms You'll Ever Need (2E)	$19.95	___
___	1-57071-346-4	Most Valuable Corporate Forms You'll Ever Need (2E)	$24.95	___
___	1-57071-347-2	Most Valuable Personal Legal Forms You'll Ever Need	$14.95	___
___	1-57071-348-0	The Power of Attorney Handbook (3E)	$19.95	___
___	1-57071-337-5	Social Security Benefits Handbook (2E)	$14.95	___
___	1-57071-354-5	U.S.A. Immigration Guide (3E)	$19.95	___
		CALIFORNIA FRONTLIST		
___	1-57071-360-X	CA Power of Attorney Handbook	$12.95	___
___	1-57071-355-3	How to File for Divorce in CA	$19.95	___
___	1-57071-356-1	How to Make a CA Will	$12.95	___
___	1-57071-357-X	How to Start a Business in CA	$16.95	___
___	1-57071-358-8	How to Win in Small Claims Court in CA	$14.95	___
___	1-57071-359-6	Landlords' Rights and Duties in CA	$19.95	___
		FLORIDA FRONTLIST		
___	1-57071-363-4	Florida Power of Attorney Handbook (2E)	$12.95	___
___	1-57071-361-8	How to Make a FL Will (5E)	$12.95	___
___	1-57071-364-2	How to Probate an Estate in FL (3E)	$24.95	___
___	1-57071-362-6	How to Win in Small Claims Court in FL (6E)	$14.95	___

Qty	ISBN	Title	Retail	Ext.
___	1-57071-335-9	Landlords' Rights and Duties in FL (7E)	$19.95	___
___	1-57071-334-0	Land Trusts in FL (5E)	$24.95	___
		GEORGIA FRONTLIST		
___	1-57071-376-6	How to File for Divorce in GA (3E)	$19.95	___
		MASSACHUSETTS FRONTLIST		
___	1-57071-329-4	How to File for Divorce in MA (2E)	$19.95	___
		NORTH CAROLINA FRONTLIST		
___	1-57071-326-X	How to File for Divorce in NC (2E)	$19.95	___
___	1-57071-327-8	How to Make a NC Will (2E)	$12.95	___
		TEXAS FRONTLIST		
___	1-57071-330-8	How to File for Divorce in TX (2E)	$19.95	___
___	1-57071-365-0	How to Start a Business in TX (2E)	$16.95	___
		FLORIDA BACKLIST		
___	1-57248-046-7	How to File for Divorce in FL (4E)	$21.95	___
___	1-57248-004-1	How to Form a Nonprofit Corp. in FL (3E)	$19.95	___
___	0-913825-96-4	How to Form a Simple Corp. in FL (3E)	$19.95	___
___	1-57248-056-4	How to Modify Your FL Divorce Judgement (3E)	$22.95	___
___	1-57248-005-X	How to Start a Business in FL (4E)	$16.95	___
___	0-913825-73-5	Women's Legal Rights in FL	$19.95	___
		GEORGIA BACKLIST		
___	1-57248-047-5	How to Make a GA Will (2E)	$9.95	___
___	1-57248-026-2	How to Start and Run a GA Business (2E)	$18.95	___
		ILLINOIS BACKLIST		
___	1-57248-042-4	How to File for Divorce in IL	$19.95	___
___	1-57248-043-2	How to Make an IL Will	$9.95	___
___	1-57248-041-6	How to Start a Business in IL	$16.95	___
___		*Form Continued on Following Page*	**SUBTOTAL**	___